PRESENTS

Elistria Warren

Copyright © 2020 Elistria Warren

All rights reserved. This book or any portion thereof may not be reproduced, distributed, or transmitted in any form or by any means, including photocopying, recording, or other electronic or mechanical methods, without the express written permission of the publisher except in the case of brief quotations embodied in critical reviews and certain other noncommercial uses permitted by copyright law. For permissions requests, write to the publisher, addressed "Attention: Permissions Coordinator," at the address below.

Printed in the United States of America
ISBN: 978-1-7347494-1-0 (Paperback)

Library of Congress Control Number: 2020910984

Published by Cocoon to Wings Publishing
7810 Gall Blvd, #311
Zephyrhills, FL 33541
www.StephanieOutten.com
(813) 906-WING (9464)

Scriptures marked NLT are taken from the HOLY BIBLE NEW LIVING TRANSLATION (NLT): Scriptures taken from the HOLY BIBLE, NEW LIVING TRANSLATION, Copyright ©1996, 2000, 2002, 2003 by Holman Bible Publishers, Nashville Tennessee. All rights reserved.

Scriptures marked NIV are taken from the NEW INTERNATIONAL VERSION (NIV): Scripture taken from THE HOLY BIBLE, NEW INTERNATIONAL VERSION® Copyright ©1973, 1978, 1984, 2011 by Biblica, Inc.™ Used by permission of Zondervan

Scriptures marked ISV are taken from the INTERNATIONAL STANDARD VERSION (ISV): Scripture taken from INTERNATIONAL STANDARD VERSION, copyright© 1996-2008 by the ISV Foundation. All rights reserved internationally.

Scriptures marked KJV are taken from the KING JAMES VERSION (KJV): KING JAMES VERSION, public domain.

Scriptures marked HCSB are taken from the HOLMAN CHRISTIAN STANDARD BIBLE (HCSB): Scripture taken from the HOLMAN CHRISTIAN STANDARD BIBLE, copyright ©1999, 2000, 2002, 2003 by Holman Bible Publishers, Nashville Tennessee. All rights reserved.

Scriptures marked ESV are taken from the THE HOLY BIBLE, ENGLISH STANDARD VERSION (ESV): Scriptures taken from THE HOLY BIBLE, ENGLISH STANDARD VERSION ® Copyright© 2001 by Crossway, a publishing ministry of Good News Publishers. Used by permission.

Scriptures marked WEB are taken from the THE WORLD ENGLISH BIBLE (WEB): WORLD ENGLISH BIBLE, public domain.

The Holy Bible, Berean Study Bible, BSB Copyright ©2016, 2018 by Bible Hub Used by Permission. All Rights Reserved Worldwide.

Scripture quotations marked (GNT) are from the Good News Translation in Today's English Version- Second Edition Copyright © 1992 by American Bible Society. Used by Permission.

GOD'S WORD is a copyrighted work of God's Word to the Nations. Quotations are used by permission. Copyright 1995 by God's Word to the Nations. All rights reserved.

Book design by Ereka Thomas Designs

Contents

Thanksgiving 1

My Story 3

Introduction 13

GOD'S PLAN 19

    The Heart of God 21

    Hunger and Thirst 33

    Set Apart 47

OPEN THE EYES OF YOUR HEART 61

    My Body: The Living Sacrifice 63

    Cleansing: Set your affections on things above 75

    Discipline 89

FIT FOR BATTLE: ARMOR ON 109

    Temptation 111

    Walk it Out 131

Next Steps 147

References 149

Thanksgiving

Abba,

What can I say? I am in awe of YOU and your continued mighty acts. I can do NOTHING without you, and I give you ALL the glory for every victory won, every chain loosed, every kingdom brought down and yoke destroyed in my life. ONLY YOU could have done this for me.

I love You! I praise You! I thank You!

To my publisher, Stephanie Outten of Cocoon to Wings Publishing

Words cannot express the depths of gratitude I have to God for you. You have been a source of strength, encouragement, maturation, and evolutionary thought. I didn't imagine this happening for me, but you helped me to see myself as the Master designed. Your expertise was exactly what I needed to birth this baby. I learned so much more about myself through the process. I have truly been transformed inside the cocoon. Now I have wings.
Thank You!

My Story

My *story begins as* a chubby little chocolate baby born in the sweltering heat of the summer in the newness of a decade. Born into a household that was plagued by fear, control, low self-worth, perversion, anger, abuse, distrust, and addiction; I was sure to have an interesting upbringing. As circumstances would have it, I encountered trauma, abuse, rejection, depression, and a host of other entanglements from childhood into my adult years. So much so that I was unaware of the level of the damage my soul had incurred until I began purposely pursuing healing. That process led me back to the root of what I now recognize as addiction. You see food became a joy, a comfort, a friend to a very confused, lonely, and desperate soul inside the body of a rejected little girl. Without the affirmation, security, and protection children need for proper social and emotional development, I reached toward what was available…FOOD.

It didn't take long for me to learn *how* to *use* food as therapy. After all, my DNA was rampant with addictions and proclivities of all sorts. All I had to do was watch, listen, and repeat. With language like, "I'll eat a brownie and I'll feel better," "I need a drink," and, "I need to get me some," saturating my atmosphere and frequently passing through my gates, the seeds were already sewn into the soil of my soul. I knew what to do. I just put it into practice. I began to sneak into the kitchen and eat food. I would squeeze next to the refrigerator so no one could see me from the door and stand there eating until I heard someone coming. I became an expert at opening the refrigerator door quietly so I could make my transactions in privacy.

I have a memory of going to the pantry and visibly seeing that the pack of cinnamon sugar graham crackers had been eaten by a rat, but I wanted them. So, I convinced myself it was just some sort of defect and I ate the crackers anyway. I stood in the doorway of our makeshift pantry, and I had a conversation with myself to reinforce the impossibility of rodent activity. As I recount this tale of desperation to you, I can see myself standing in the kitchen of my childhood home, in front of that wooden makeshift pantry talking myself into eating those graham crackers. I can see the indentations in the corner of the crackers; they had hardened around the edges. The rat's saliva, mixed with cinnamon and sugar, sat on the surface of the crackers long enough to dry in the humid air of our concrete house; that's how the crust formed. My addiction was so strong before the age of ten that I willfully exposed myself to potential disease instead of missing out on my fix. The kicker is I wasn't even hungry. I just WANTED to eat. You see an addict will go to whatever lengths necessary to achieve their goal of euphoria. The mind will create whatever reality necessary to support addiction.

My addiction persisted into my adolescent and teen years. In addition to my parents separating, I endured bullying in the forms of social, emotional, verbal, and sometimes physical abuse on a daily basis in my educational and extracurricular settings. I found very little comfort during these years. Peers and adults, who were tasked with being my guardians and protectors, inflicted the abuse and trauma on me. The teachers and administrators offered little assistance, and I found no help in certain family members because they were a part of the popular group and didn't want me to do anything to disrupt their place in the pecking order. I felt very alone, so food became an even closer friend, especially during a time of extreme poverty our family experienced. We survived an entire summer on drop biscuits and Kool-Aid. My mother supported our newly broken home with her teaching assistant salary and whatever she could borrow or get from pawning her jewelry. It was a very difficult time in our lives, but our bellies were full, and we made the best of it. With emotional highs and lows creeping around every corner with notices of eviction, loss of utilities, or threats of physical harm from a semi-present father, I sank further into the pit of addiction. But I didn't know that at the time.

All I knew was that I had become an expert at making biscuits and began to crave the flavor of them. Food was my best friend, and I wanted it around me all the time. I wanted to see it and would frequently go to the kitchen to check the pantry and refrigerator to make sure I had what I needed for my next fix. It didn't matter if I was hungry or not. I NEEDED to know what I saw a moment ago was still there. Poverty reinforced my addictions by moving food from the place of novelty and desire to the place of need, comfort, and peace. My world was exploding around me, but I was inside a bubble feeling joy and happiness when I ate. It was me and my friend. I didn't hear my mother crying in the next room, my brother being beaten, or the sounds of the neighborhood. I retreated into myself and ate my cares away. I couldn't tell anyone what my life was really like. I was well indoctrinated with the philosophy of "what happens in this house stays in this house!" So, I ate. I ate to fill the void in my soul created by years of persistent, successive trauma.

As an older teen, the dynamic of my addiction shifted. I no longer needed someone else to prepare meals for me, I could create them on my own. When I began working and earning my own income, I could then afford the fast food and novelty foods I always wanted as a child. My treasure was made evident by how I allocated my income. Food became my top priority. After having suffered through periods of poverty and lack, I was excited to have the resources to buy the food I wanted to eat...even those I was allergic to. It didn't matter because my goal was to eat and eat whatever *I* wanted. No one could tell me "NO" because I purchased it with my own money. And, if they did, I would sneak off and eat it anyway. Snacks, cookies, chips, pretzels, all manners of sweets, chocolate, breads, and cakes. You name it, and I got it. My little grocery store paycheck would be gone in no time. Thrown away on massive quantities of sugar, salt, and preservatives.

These behaviors continued and progressed in strength into my adulthood. Though I had brief stints of 'health kicks,' I would always return to my vomit; repeating cycles of old behaviors that led to excessive eating. I would have success until an emotional trigger occurred; then it was a complete wash. I had no tools to combat the emotional rollercoaster of disappointment and hurt so I ate to quiet the whispers of self-loathing and images of rehearsed offenses. With each recount, the flavors, desires, fantasies, and imaginations of the 'joy' I felt when eating came flooding back. I simply surrendered to the unction. I would frequently wake in the middle of the night to use the restroom and stand up, half asleep, literally stuffing my face full of whatever I had on hand. And, if I didn't have it, I would get dressed and leave my house at all times of night. I drove great distances to get my fix. It didn't matter if it was two miles or twenty, I went the distance to meet my emotional needs.

After successive rejections, abandonments, betrayals, relational traumas and abuses, food was no longer a comfort or friend, it was a whole IDOL. This idol was built on the firm foundation of a Grand Canyon-sized void in my soul, a chasm of despair and hopelessness. I could go weeks without quality personal human interactions because my life was built around an altar to food. My work schedule, clients, outings, personal appointments, and daily life centered around where and what I would eat that day. Pay days were the climax because I had an abundance of resources to purchase the best sacrifices to place on the altar. I justified my addiction by labeling it therapy, comfort, peace, happiness, fellowship, hanging out, and fun. But the reality was that I didn't need an occasion; I made daily offerings to my idol. I never left a stale sacrifice on the altar; I was devout in my service to my flesh. My daily devotions were plentiful and varied. Salty, sweet, tangy, tart, crunchy, crispy, soft, doughy, hot, cold, and lukewarm. I offered the very best to my idol...no slacking! I was fully committed. I gathered my offerings from near and far, some of which were eaten while driving to acquire the next. I would hardly make it out of the parking lot of the store before I had bags and boxes open, fingers sticky and covered in the evidence of my addiction. I knew the best times of day to purchase my offerings of the freshest and highest quality product. I woke early to be sure I got the crispy, warm, glazed croissants from the grocery store. I knew what days the stores received their shipments so I would avoid stale sacrifices. I knew the faces of the culinary staff that produced the best results. If they weren't there, I didn't want it. I had a well-established devotional and worship routine. Especially when my monthly cycle was approaching. I didn't wait for the cravings to hit, I went directly to the store to buy a strawberry soda, chips, and cream-filled chocolate snack cakes. I memorized the required sacrifice schedule. I knew when pizza, ice cream, brownies, pickles, or chocolate were required. I knew what friend to call when each sacrifice was due on the altar. If none were available, it didn't matter. I knew how to worship on my own. I didn't need any help!

There was one particular time of many in my life where I was repeating a cycle of poverty and was struggling financially. I went to a local agency to get assistance with paying my rent. I was denied. The social servant told me very plainly that I made enough money to pay all my bills and did not qualify for their program. I sat there confused because I knew I had zero dollars in my bank account. She sat at her desk working and never looked at me again. I sat there for a few more moments still confused and then left angry. I got up early, stood in line for hours, endured the Florida heat, and then she had the nerve to tell me no... I was HOT!!! A short while later I met with a financial planner who bluntly told me, "you spend all your money on food. You need to stop eating out so much." I was astonished! I had no idea that my financial struggle was empowered by my addiction. I was completely ignorant of the word God gave in Proverbs 23:21 that clearly states that gluttons will live in poverty. That was the moment I recognized the severity of my dependency. I was literally eating myself out of house and home. I thought I just liked to eat, I didn't know that the desire was depleting my resources and depriving me of the security of having my basic needs met. My addiction took precedence over having shelter, made evident by my bank statements. My treasure was food, and my heart was loyal to a fault.

Addiction can be defined as compulsive inclinations toward a person, place, or thing. Yes, ladies and gentlemen, you can be addicted to more than drugs and alcohol. Addiction is indiscriminate and affects hearts across socio-economic status, culture, continent, and color. From the suburbs to the housing projects of any city, addiction can be found there. I had a HUGE altar built to food in my heart and I was completely unaware of it. I was an addict! I didn't shoot up into my veins or snort up my nostrils; my dispensers were a fork and knife.

All these outcomes lent themselves to my formidable, pervasive, and perpetual addictions. Yes! Food was simply one facet of the hard stone of addiction in my heart. You see, addiction is prevalent in the paternal and maternal lineage of my family, in both males and females. Prior to my healing journey, I identified addiction as heavy use of illegal substances or related to pornography. The truth of God's word and the revelation of His Holy Spirit taught me to remove the veils and see myself as I was...broken. But, that's not the end of the story! God loved me through and placed people along my path to assist me through the wilderness and help me untangle the mess in my soul. Through my commitment to the process of deliverance and inner healing, I am now in a state of freedom and assisting others to navigate the maze of deliverance and walk into freedom.

Introduction

Chiiiiiiiillllleeee, look here!! Congratulations! Not only have you purchased the book, but you actually opened it and are reading. Praise God! You are embarking on a journey toward health and wholeness. The whirlwinds of life have turned you toward the path of hope and help for change. You've already read my story. Now, allow me to introduce myself. My name is Elistria Warren, and I will be your guide. As the founder, owner, and visionary of Thee Gold Standard, LLC, I am honored to be your trusted navigator. The Holy Spirit will be your compass as you sojourn through the recesses of your heart to find the roots of your inordinate affection for food.

We will work together to help you identify the genesis of your relationship with and view of food. This journal will provide you with opportunities to know yourself on deeper levels. The exercises, writing prompts, and commentary are designed to assist you with self-exploration at levels you never thought possible. Each activity was crafted to facilitate the strategic unveiling of triggers. These triggers incite the behaviors and mindsets that ensure your pervasive dependency upon food to regulate your emotional, soulish, physical, and spiritual deficits. I know...you didn't think it would get that deep. Trust me, it gets deeper.

As a veteran social worker who spent fifteen years as a home service provider and educational facilitator, I have been fortunate to view the seeding, nurturing, and fostering of every kind of social, emotional, economic, spiritual, physical, dietary, and financial dysfunction known to man. I began my career as a case manager to pregnant and parenting teens. During this time, to better meet the needs of my clients, I became a certified childbirth educator (CBE), lactation consultant (CLC), certified youth worker, and a newborn care educator. In addition to serving as a home visitor, I also provided support to families in the obstetric/pediatric and community settings as a group facilitator. I later transitioned to assisting the families of children with special needs as a resource advocate and infant toddler developmental specialist (ITDS); providing one-on-one therapeutic and coaching sessions. Rounding out my decade-long tenure took me back to pregnancy-related services that extended from the child's birth to age three. When that phase of my career ended, I entered the world of educational case management. This unique placement allowed me to see the results of families' missed opportunities to form core values; instead, I sadly saw the continuation of generationally-appropriated and learned behaviors that perpetuate cycles of bondage.

I crossed paths with some families many times across service genres...chains still heavy, bondages unbroken, and strongholds firmly rooted. However, there were families that excelled with the acceptance of wise counsel; going on to obtain degrees of elevation far above the chains of their past, choices, and ancestry.

Social work provided me the unique opportunity to 'travel the world' without ever leaving my city. I engaged belief systems, mindsets, social customs, and paradigms across socio-economic, cultural, religious, geographical, racial, ethnic, and identities. I can say that I have literally seen and heard it all...just about. After all, there really is *NOTHING* new under the sun (Ecclesiastes 1:9). From the back roads to the country clubs and private property, I have served the people and seen the results of addictions of every kind.

The core of your self-exploration will be aided by studying the lives of two characters, Auntie and her niece, Tonya. Their experiences will assist you with discovering and understanding how addiction manifests and the variety of methods they use to remain in control and dominate your existence. If you haven't realized it by now, food is RULING your life! There are literal chains surrounding you in the spirit, and they are preventing you from walking into freedom. One week in the life of our two characters will demonstrate just how potent and intoxicating the foul waters of addiction are that flow within your soul.

Your decision to open this book and read it means that you are closer than you think to a life free from dependency on food. To finish a journey, one must first begin. This journal is designed to get you out of the 'starter blocks' and onto the track toward freedom. I will walk you through the process Abba (God as Father) took me through to obtain the free gift of healing. Much of what I will share with you are the strategies, techniques, and disciplines the Holy Spirit gave me to ensure my success in the process of coming to healing and wholeness; along with a few tips and tricks I gleaned along my journey.

As we sojourn through the text, you will become aware of your historical relationship with food and determine the course of that future. You will also become aware of the familial, regional, and cultural norms that have kept you in bondage due to expectation and opinion. The text will coach you through how to identify the doors through which addiction entered your soul and explain how to close them. Identifying points of entry is vitally important to NOT continuing cycles after achieving deliverance.

Let's get started!

For Journal Prompt exercises, if additional lines are needed for responses, use Notes Pages at the back of the book.

God's Plan

The Heart of God

Auntie: I am so proud of you! You are taking over the role of making our family's famous peach cobbler for the annual church picnic. It's the best in all the land! I can't wait to taste it.

Tonya: Aaaawwww...OMG! Thanks Auntie! I'm so excited, I worked really hard. It's my first time, so I hope everyone loves it as much as they love yours every year.

Auntie: I'm sure they will, honey. This recipe has been in our family for 20 years. We win the prize every year! Everyone knows that we have the best peach cobbler [Auntie winks at a passerby].

Tonya: Oh yes! I'm sure, Auntie. I made just a few small improvements. I hope everyone loves it.

Auntie: [Auntie turns around slowly from arranging the display with a look of strong concern on her face] Improvements? What improvements can you make to perfection, sweetheart? Our family recipe has won the Blue Ribbon for the last 20 years straight. What changes could you possibly have made? [Auntie stands with arms folded while waiting for the earth-shattering answer.]

Tonya: [Cheesing with excitement she explains,] Oh! Well, my boyfriend is Asian so I added a little sesame oil so he could have a familiar flavor. We LOOOVVVEEEE sesame oil. It's so yummy. And, then my best friend, she's from Bangladesh, so I added in a little cardamom. She's been homesick and I know that it will just bless her heart to have some flavors of home. We drink this Chai tea that has cardamom in it. Have you ev--

Auntie: [In an elevated tone with matching body language, Auntie cuts off Tonya] Have you lost your mind?!?!?!?

Tonya: [Startled by Auntie's change in tone and posture, Tonya leans back and hesitates to respond] Wha-what do you mean, Auntie? I was just adding in some international flavors. I know everyone will love it. With the college and all the new people coming to town and all. Besides Auntie, doesn't the Bible say something about going into all the world--

Auntie: [With closed eyes Auntie exclaims] Gal! SHUT UP!!! [picture aggressive hand gestures and fierce eyes] What does that have to do with my grandmama's recipe that you done tor' up? Do you really think we gon' win now????? Grrrrr

Tonya: I didn't destroy it, Auntie. I just made some improvements. What's wrong with that? Don't we always want to get better?

[Auntie exits stage left FUMING hot about that recipe while Tonya stands pitifully confused with her pan of cobbler watching Auntie storm off whispering expletives into the breeze.]

Tonya: I don't see the problem? What's wrong with a little cultural flavor? I bet it's delicious. Let me get a spoon. [Big

> spoonful down the hatch…chew…swallow…smirk of assurance melts from her face…a raised head reveals enlarged eyes…a strong gaze back down at her masterpiece] Eew! Dis nasty!

It may seem petty to be upset about not winning a blue ribbon, but the principle of the matter is this: when you've been given a recipe for success and you change it, it's unlikely that you will achieve the same result. Abba gave us an airtight construct (recipe) for health and prosperity in the garden. Very specific instructions were provided AND He conveniently gave us all the ingredients we would need in one location. When ingredients were added and changes were made, *then* we see, and are still experiencing, the effects of not following the recipe.

LET'S TALK ABOUT IT!

As parents, we want the best for our children. We spend an indeterminable amount of time planning events, choosing homes, buying clothing, researching the best methods of doing X, Y, and Z all centered around what's best for them. Some go so far as to choose their career path and the region of the country or world they will reside in based on the caliber of schools and/or the family friendliness rating. Why? Because we want the very best for our children. Parents want to provide their children with the best opportunities for success.

When children first come into the world, they are helpless and totally dependent upon their parents for survival; namely Mother. Her womb was considered home during their hopefully 40-week gestation, and for a newborn, Mother's body is so intricately designed by Abba to meet all their needs that her body will alter its temperature to make sure that the baby remains warm. Her breasts will produce the perfect amount of colostrum and milk of an exact composition to meet the child's nutritional needs on demand. This milk is so easily digested that baby's bowels move frequently without strain or discomfort. The length of her arm is perfect to hold her new baby and provide the nurture and comforting necessary for growth and development. The distance of her face from the gaze of her infant is exact to promote bonding and attachment. In moments of frustration and discomfort the sound of her voice soothes her infant. Due to infant's eyesight slowly developing and preferring round shapes of dark and light variance, Abba perfectly designed the shape of the mother's face, eyes, mouth, and breasts to draw the attention of the baby. This design makes certain that baby will be inclined to look upon that which will preserve their life.

Abba did the same for man when He created and placed them in the Garden. He provided a perfect climate made evident by their comfort in being naked in the garden. If it were cold, I'm sure Abba would've inspired them at some point to put some clothes on. I don't know where they would have come from. Maybe some flax or hemp threads. Perhaps He could have commanded a few silkworms to weave a robe up in there somewhere. Who knows? But I digress. The point is that a perfect environment was created for them that met all their needs. Abba even provided them with a dietary construct that was perfect in its composition, just like mother's milk.

Genesis 1:29-30 (NIV) states,

> "Then God said, 'I give you every seed-bearing plant on the face of the whole earth and every tree that has fruit with seed in it. They will be yours for food. And to all the beasts of the earth and all the birds in the sky and all the creatures that move along the ground-everything that has the breath of life in it-I give every green plant for food.' And it was so."

As we have read, Abba gave clear instruction on what He intended and designed for man to eat. Not only man, but every creature with the breath of God in it. Lions, tigers, and bears were also plant eaters. Oh my!!! Yes, ladies and gentlemen, nothing on the face of the earth ate meat at creation. Elohim (The Creator) in His wisdom and perfect plan created ALL living beings to live and be nourished by a diet that consisted of plants. Pause, lift your chin off the floor, close your mouth, let the blood come back to your face, unclench your fists, loosen up your shoulders, and take a few deep breaths. Relax. If you want to reference a few other translations to be sure it's not a fluke, go ahead. I did. When I first read this in the text I was astounded! No one had ever read the book of Genesis to me or given me any instructions from this chapter regarding my lifestyle and how I was to live. I'd always been told that Genesis 1 was about the creation of man. It was not until I began to walk the road of healing that I began to read with new eyes and have an understanding that the WHOLE Bible is profitable to us to learn optimal guidelines for living an abundant life.

Eden was flawless. He loves us so much that He created a perfect garden and planted us in it to ensure our optimal development. A paradise representative of Abba's desire for man to abide with Him, in His image, in His context of pristine abundance and beauty. Just as Abba created the Mother's body to foster the growth and maturation of the child and later to produce perfectly comprised milk for the absolute benefit and thriving of the newborn, so too did

He bring forth man from the womb of the earth and create an environment consistent of everything man would need for complete nourishment. In the garden, He surrounded man with vegetables, fruit, trees, and plants that brought forth all manner of vegetation for food. There was nothing lacking in this place of perfection and everything in it was designed to meet the needs of all creation.

There are those that present arguments of "Jesus ate fish," and "the Israelites ate meat," and "they sacrificed lambs on the altar," to support the consumption of meat. All these statements are true; however, they are out of context regarding this commentary. The arguments are also without consideration of the *original* intent of the Father. The story of Noah teaches us that prior to the flood and the subsiding of the waters, men did not eat meat.

Genesis 9:3 (NIV) states,

> "Everything that lives and moves about will be food for you. Just as I gave you the green plants, I now give you everything."

After sin entered the earth and man became cursed, Adam and Eve were cast out of the garden forbidden to return. The Bible tells of the further degeneration of the moral character of man. Then we see God determined to destroy the earth and its inhabitants due to their depravity. Prior to *all* these occurrences, man did not eat meat nor was he intended to. If man had not sinned against God by eating the fruit of The Tree of the Knowledge of Good and Evil, he would have never left the garden. Thus, meat consumption would never have entered the dietary construct of man, and all of creation would still be walking around naked, in the cool breeze, talking with God, and eating an organic, naturally gluten free, vegan diet. LOL

The story of Noah also provides us with a symbol of God's promise. (Genesis 9:13) The rainbow is a sign from God that he has Covenant with man in the earth. A covenant is a promise, a contract, an agreement between the parties with specific conditions and terms of relationship. Today when we see a rainbow, the promise remains that God will never again destroy the Earth with a flood. Though this promise is not related to a dietary construct, I utilize the rainbow as a symbol of a promise of good health for those I influence. 3 John 1:2 teaches us about God's heart toward His children. Though this is not a red-letter scripture, meaning that Jesus said it directly, 2 Timothy 3:16 informs the reader that all scriptures should and can be used to instruct us in righteousness and correct living. Abba wants us to prosper in every area of life; our health, finances, relationships, and profession. Abba's heart's desire is that we be prosperous and reflect His glory in every scenario, at all times.

I encourage you to eat the rainbow. What does that mean? It means that your food intake should mimic the color range of the rainbow. I frequently use this motto:

Color = nutrients   Color = flavor

When our plate resembles the bow of promise, we are partaking in the promise of God for health and prosperity. From this viewpoint, the rainbow represents the fullness of variety of the plants, trees, fruit, vegetables, and every green plant that Abba gave us in the garden for our meat.

I encourage you to view your health as a part of your wealth. Most people would view monetary wealth as a part of the prosperous life. However, I encourage you to view your physical health as a part of that promise as well. Each choice you make to have a healthy meal or adopt a habit to improve your health is like an endowment toward your account. Continual deposits grow the balance (wealth) and increase your likelihood of comfort in your later years. What good would it do you to gain great riches if you were too sick and diseased to enjoy it?

LET'S WORK THROUGH THIS TOGETHER

Prompts:

1. Did you know this dietary construct was present in the FIRST chapter of the Bible? How do you feel now that you have discovered it?

   _____
   _____
   _____
   _____

2. How do you feel about what you've learned? Sad, Happy, Joy, conviction, clarity, confirmation? WHY? Describe your feelings.

   _____
   _____
   _____
   _____

3. How do you think your life would be as a resident in the garden as Abba originally intended?

   _____
   _____
   _____
   _____

Encouragement:

Thankfully, God is the only one that is Omniscient (knows all things). He reveals everything to us in the time that we can acknowledge, receive, accept, and act. There is no need to feel down or deficient in your faith because you didn't know this vital information; or that you knew and didn't take action. I lived most of my life without this revelation. Good news! The word of God teaches us that there is no condemnation for those who are in Christ Jesus (Romans 8:1). Praise God! There is no room for guilt or shame in the paradigm of the Kingdom. God's grace is sufficient for everything that we can ever encounter. The question now is, what are you going to do now that you know?

If you are reading this journal and you are not a believer in the Lord Jesus Christ, my hope for you is that as you turn the pages, and the careful plans the Father has taken to ensure your safety and success are revealed, this journal will enlighten you to your acceptance in the Father's heart. He has a place, a plan, and a perfect will for your life as well. I pray that this journal will give you a glimpse into that reality.

Prayer:

Elohim, you are so awesome. You so carefully constructed the world and all of its contents to birth us into perfection. Thank you for your love for us. You knew exactly what was needed to keep us on the path to complete health, wealth, and prosperity. You created us to fit perfectly into your puzzle of creation. Now that your perfect will has been revealed to me, help me to adapt and make the changes necessary to return to your plan of perfection. I want my will to be in line with your perfect will. I can only do this with your help. Help me, Abba!

In Jesus name, Amen

Hunger and Thirst

Scenario: It's 5:30 p.m. on a Tuesday evening. Tonya has had a rough day at work and is still recovering from the run-in she had with Auntie at the church picnic this weekend. Auntie is still a little upset about that cobbler and is not returning Tonya's calls or texts. Auntie is normally the person Tonya goes to for wisdom and guidance when life is out of whack, but she does not have that resource at this time. Let's see how she is managing.

[Tonya walks in and plops down on the couch after work.] This woman really tried me today. I'm saved, but I ain't that saved!!! She can get the ministry of the laying on of hands, in Jesus Name! Then we can pray the healing virtue of the Lord down. OK! [Deep breath, insert self-regulating hand gesture here] Put the sword away Peter. Tonya, get it together. God ain't pleased with that.

Lord have Mercy! Where is my phone?!?!? Why isn't she texting me back? I need to talk to her! Where is that brownie I bought yesterday? [She digs through her purse to find her 'just in case' snack.] Aaaaahhhhh! Yaaasssss! Praise G-...Bless His name. [Hardly chewing and swallowing the massive brownie, she checks her messages to see if her boyfriend has responded to her voicemail.] Where he at? I texted him twice today. I know good and well he can't be that busy [insert eye roll and a good ole fashioned huff].

[It's now 6:16 p.m. In Tonya's mind, everyone has had plenty of time to get through traffic, get home, get a snack, have a beverage, check their messages, and call her with agreement regarding her work scenario. While opening a family-sized bag of Sour Cream and Cheddar chips, she dials her best friend.] Uuggghhhh! Why is no one answering the phone!?!?! [Licking her fingers, she scrolls through her contacts to see who else might be a good counselor in this moment.] No ma'am, not her. She just got fired for stealing boxes from work...who does that? [Scroll] Oh, un uh! Not him. He got a crush on me. If he come up and through here, it's gon' be a situation. [Insert enlarged eyes and a head cocked to the side]. I don't even know why his number is still in my phone, but I'll hold onto it in case he needs me to pray for him. [Still smacking and scrolling] Heck No!!!! I can't deal with Momma right now. All she wants to talk about is my brother. I don't wanna hear that.

[It's now 8 p.m. and no one has responded to her outreach. Tonya has accomplished nothing on her to-do list and has, instead, spent her entire evening eating and feeling *dropped* by her support system. She has eaten a large brownie, drank a glass of wine, taken a Xanax, eaten half of a party-sized bag of chips, masturbated, eaten the remainder of her Chinese food from lunch at the mall, and still doesn't *feel* satisfied. Sitting on the couch and eating the remainder of a bag of spicy pork rinds she had earlier, she comes to a conclusion] [slamming her phone down on the couch] I'm sick of these raggedy folks! I'm there for them and when I need to talk ain't nobody around?!?! Whateva! [insert hand gesture here]

> Imma get this good dulce de leche out the freezer, order me a pizza with that good cheesy garlic pan crust. OK! Pop me in a movie, and it's gon' be alright. I don't need nobody. God got me!!! It's me and you, Jesus. (Looking and pointing up to the ceiling) [She folds her arms across her chest while she retrieves the delivery number from her speed dial.]

It is in our moments of weakness, hurt, distress, dis-ease, and frustration that the truest intents and contents of our hearts are revealed. When we lack the comfort and support we so desperately desire, the hidden portions of our psyche are exposed. When the fabric is stretched, the body behind it is revealed. The flaws, wounds, and gaping holes begin to surface when we are denied what we desire or feel we deserve. There is a formula for exposing the truth:

Tired + Hurt + Hungry = *(Truth Revealed)*

LET'S TALK ABOUT IT!

Coping skills are vital to the human experience. Coping skills are methods or strategies we use to help us deal with stressors in our environment. This environment can be inward or outward, natural or spiritual. We learn and develop these skills from the womb. Thousands of utero photos of fetuses sucking their thumbs, a comforting and self-regulating behavior, are present on web pages around the world. The information age gives us access to a wealth of knowledge that increases our understanding. We can view the transformative process of a sperm into a newborn baby, the pollination of our favorite flower, or the mating habits of wildebeests on the Serengeti in a matter of seconds. We have the privilege and honor of watching the development of a generation before our very eyes. This allows us to have hindsight that is greater than 20/20 and look retroactively at ourselves and how we came to our current state of being.

Coping skills are important but must be kept in proper perspective. It is important that we have several so that we can rotate according to the situation we are dealing with. However, it is important to ensure that our coping skills are healthy and do not lead to further damage. Consider the parent who wants their child to stop sucking their thumb. Why is this a problem? Hands in the mouth increase exposure to potentially harmful bacteria, viruses, germs, and substances. The parent's concern is for the health of the child, and this is why great care is taken to cease the behavior. The parent knows the danger of continuing the behavior and wants to prevent the child from adverse effects. There is a very lucrative industry built on the desire of parents who want their children to develop healthily. Countless resources exist to assist parents and children with learning appropriate methods of soothing, care, and development. Knowing this about our natural parents, wouldn't we believe that our heavenly Father desires much more for us to develop healthy coping skills? To prevent us from experiencing the contamination of the lust of the flesh, the lust of the eyes, and the Pride of life? It is integral to our walk with God that we learn and develop our view of Him as our comforter. Faith and Trust in Him to supply and meet all our needs is *THE* coping strategy of the Kingdom. If we seek to be satisfied by any other source, we enter into idolatry and are ingesting the contaminations of sin.

Young children learn to rock themselves if they are not held and cuddled, meeting the basic human need we have for nurturing. If there is no response to their cry, a child will cease to use their God-given alarm system for receiving care. Countless studies have been performed, proving that food, shelter, and clothing are not enough to secure the developmental milestones needed for complete maturation. The nurture is of even greater importance as nature to healthy development of the human body and soul.

Soap Box Side Note: You don't have a "good baby" because they don't cry. You have a baby that has learned that you won't meet their need, so they cease attempts to have it met. Sounds like adults in unhealthy relationships, huh? Right! Like I said, we learn before we can comprehend our actions for how to respond when a need has been neglected.

> In Psalms 3:4-6 (KJV) David writes, "I cried unto the LORD with my voice, and he heard me out of His holy hill. Selah. I laid me down and slept; I awaked; for the LORD sustained me."

This Scripture paints a beautiful picture of how Abba nurtures us and meets our basic and deepest needs. When we cry out, He promises to hear and respond. Too often we look to man to fulfill the needs that only a Holy God can minister to. This breeds disappointment and sows vast fields from seeds of resentment, anger, fear, and hurt that can yield a crop the size of Pharaoh's army. The good news is that God defeated Pharaoh's army and He is more than able to defeat the insurgents upon your soul if you are willing and obedient.

In the above scenario Tonya can be compared to the woman at the well. When she encounters Jesus, He makes it clear to her that she has had five husbands and is still unfulfilled in her current situation. Tonya went from person to person and snack to snack never having her need met. She threw in a little acknowledgement of God but never came to the place where she recognized, received, and acted upon the revelation of God as El Shaddai (the all sufficient God, the multi breasted one). She chose to seek out satisfaction from her cocktail of vices but at the end of the day was still dissatisfied and attempted to fill that wound with junk food. She chose to worship food instead of worshipping the Father. He inhabits the praises of His people. The appropriate response to distress is worship! Seeking the face and the heart of the Father would have brought her to a place of peace in the midst of the storm.

In my past there have been many times, too numerous to count, where I have found myself in Tonya's position. I desperately sought water from wells that had no capacity to fill me or to satisfy the longing in my soul. On the contrary, they were filled with rancid water that was diseased and full of death. There were long standing voids in my soul that I attempted to fill with every dessert, snack, and novelty food item I could gather enough funds to purchase. The cultural favorites and trips to my favorite restaurants would not only tip the scale of my heart past gluttony toward obsession and addiction, but to my dismay, toward abuse.

Abuse is a strong word, but it is accurate for the lifestyle and practices I had in place for decades. I was in an abusive relationship with food. Merriam-Webster dictionary online (2020) defines abuse as:

- "improper or excessive use or treatment: MISUSE
- language that condemns or vilifies usually unjustly, intemperately, and angrily
- physical maltreatment"

Based on these definitions and the description of my relationship with food, one could conclude that my abuse of food led to its effects abusing me. From frequent allergic reactions that led to consistent and excessive use of creams, liquids, and pills to calm the uncontrollable itching, welts, and rashes; to the excruciating bouts of constipation and diarrhea, to which my response was to take laxatives and/or eat more food to "push it out," I felt the effects. To the violent episodes of diarrhea that caused dehydration and rapid drops in electrolytes that caused dizziness and light-headedness, to which my response was to eat more food to "stop it up," I felt the effects. To the poverty enabling behaviors of shopping at convenience locations to get the 'familiar' foods and flavors that my addiction demanded on a daily basis; to the resulting bouts of depression when my finances ran out and I had no clothes to wear because my body had grown too wide and my belly had swollen beyond the reach of the elastic in my pants. To the frequent checking of my account balance to be sure I had enough to buy that pack of cookies, ice cream sandwich, bags of chips, hot dog, chili cheese nachos, hit the drive-thru to get those fresh fries out the oil... to the planning of my schedule to beat the line at my favorite sweet shop or chicken joint, my God. To rearranging my work schedule to ensure I was on the right side of town on the days my suppliers had their specials...I told you and I meant it...food told me what to do and I, so I thought, had no choice but to obey. When I came to moments of clarity, I would make promises and vow to change but I had no willpower or tools in place to assist me beyond short lived success. So, after a period of time, triggers arose that would build tension and inevitably I would fall back into the same cycle; time after time, year after year, decade after decade. Any way you measure it, addiction and I had a very abusive relationship.

My addiction controlled me in every facet of life. It demanded my resources, made decisions on who I could spend time with, the amount of time I could designate for an event, affected my body and its functions, changed my appearance, and told me what I could wear. Afterward, I called myself names and put myself down when addiction had its way with me. You see, my inordinate affection (i.e., addiction) for food taught me how to further abuse myself. Though I began to see a pattern, I had no hope and saw no way of escape. My affections were on things of this earth and that obstructed my gaze. 1 Corinthians 10:13 teaches us that God ALWAYS provides a way of escape. Note also that this text states that the temptations we have are common. This means that the guilt, shame, and condemnation I felt after binging was a strategy of my abuser to keep me locked in a cycle of abuse. I felt that I was the only person struggling with this issue. I didn't share it with anyone or reach out for help. I did as many of you have done, suffer in silence and continue to eat my life away in the privacy and seclusion of my car, home, office, and anywhere else I could, away from the eyes of those who might judge me...continuing to hide snack wrappers, soda bottles, empty chip bags, crumbs, dropped fries, and fast food receipts. Silence was the lock that held me captive in the prison of addiction.

I recall a moment when I was at a close friend's home. We were sitting on the couch watching movies and she offered me salsa and chips. I had never had that brand before and didn't have good experiences in the past, so I was reluctant, but I tried it anyway. I can vividly remember the widening of my eyes, the awakening of my taste buds, and the excitement I felt at how good it was. It was a high I hadn't experienced before. It was new, fresh, and tasty and I wanted MORE! I began to grab chip after chip and dip it into the jar all while talking to her and explaining how delicious it was. Before I knew it, the jar was almost gone and the bag half empty. When I looked back at my friend, she had an expression on her face that I can only describe as surprisingly appalled disgust. I immediately began to sink within myself as a tsunami of emotion began to stir in my soul; a tidal wave of shame overtook me from the inside out. I told her that I would buy her more to replace it, quickly closed up the bag, and went back to my seat to watch the movie in silence. All the while stewing in a sea of shame that turned to anger. After all, she offered it to me, I didn't ask. How dare she be disgusted with me? She was the hostess and she was SUPPOSED to provide refreshments. All this commentary ran through my mind but the truth of it is I was angry that my addiction was now EXPOSED. I didn't want to be uncovered because I wasn't ready to let it go. I didn't know HOW to be free.

This is the reality for many people who struggle with food addiction. Just like the woman at the well, here I am minding my own business, thinking that I'm being polite, and she had to go and expose me to me. She had to be a mirror and show me just how depraved my soul was. How dare she be an outward manifestation of what I was inwardly feeling, thinking, and doing to myself. How dare she show me ME! Unlike Jesus, this friend exposed me but had no tools or means to help me through the process of wholeness. As one of my clients said to me, "Everyone has somewhere to go except people who struggle with food." While I understand her sentiment due to the lack of resources and community surrounding this issue, I have to disagree. Abba is our refuge in every storm. He is our safe place. He is our redeemer and He is our Healer.

He is the God who satisfies. He is El Shaddai (the multi breasted God) and Jehovah Jireh (Our Provider). All our needs, longings, and desires can only be met through relationship with Him. But, how can I drink from a well when I don't know where it is or how to get there?

Just like the woman at the well, just like Tonya, my soul was thirsting and hungering but it was not being filled. Can you see your past or current self in Tonya's actions? What about in my story?

LET'S WORK THROUGH THIS TOGETHER

Prompts:

1. How many coping mechanisms can you identify from Tonya's scenario?

   _____
   _____
   _____
   _____
   _____
   _____

2. Recall a moment in time when you had a desperate need and it was not met by the person(s) you felt responsible to do so. How did you feel?

   _____
   _____
   _____
   _____

3. Name 2 coping skills you use on a regular basis. Describe how they assist you in moments of distress? Do you feel better or worse after using them?

   _____
   _____
   _____

4. What are your vices?

   _____
   _____
   _____

5. Have you ever used food as a coping mechanism? Describe the scenario.

   _____
   _____
   _____
   _____

Encouragement:

He's a good Father. (Matthew 7:9-11). He is the well that never runs dry, and when we drink of Him we will never thirst again. (1 John 4: 13-15). He refreshes us. (Psalm 23:2). He hears and answers our call. (1 John 5:14-15). He inclines His ear to us. (Psalm 116:2). He is the bread of life and you will never be hungry again. (John 6:35). ALL that you need is within the Father's love. Trust in Him, believe His word is true, and you shall be satisfied! (Psalm 107:9).

Prayer:

Abba, your word says that whoever hungers and thirsts after righteousness shall be filled. You promised that if I drink and eat of you that I would never hunger and thirst again. I surrender my appetites, my longings and desires, my ideas of the outcomes of my life and my future, on the altar. Abba, help me to hunger and thirst for you. I only want to desire what you have purposed for me. Change my natural and spiritual taste buds to desire your bread and water. Help me to see you as you truly are - the ONLY God who satisfies.

In Jesus Name, Amen

Set Apart

Scenario: It's Tuesday evening and Auntie has been ignoring Tonya's calls and text messages all day. She feels she is justified in ignoring her because Tonya ruined the family's winning streak at the church picnic. Auntie saw this winning streak as a legacy for her and the family name. After all, with this winning streak, no one talks about the fact that her husband ran off with the pastor's daughter anymore... What will she do now?

[Auntie is having a conversation with herself to justify ignoring Tonya in a time of need. Sitting on the couch flipping through Christian Women Today's current issue, she begins to explain why she is RIGHT] (Phone buzzes for the umpteenth time) Uuuhh! Lil girl! Leave. Me. Alone! (slamming the phone down on the couch) I am not paying you any attention. What you need to do is go find my GrandMomma recipe! Text that! Do that! (Insert violent turns of the magazine pages) I don't want to hear about them raggedy people on your job. I got to be about the Lord's work, I don't have time for office gossip. (insert a pious Holy Ghost head shake with a sanctified facial expression and a raised handshake).

[Remembering that the National church convention is approaching, Auntie reacts and switches magazines]. Ahhhh! Thank ya, Holy Ghost. I need to order my outfit for

Convention next month. I got to step in there right. I represent the Kingdom of God. I can't go half steppin'. No Suh! And it got to be the right color. I refuse to be in there lookin' like Sis. Walters with all them different shades of green on. My God today. Woman of God, choose one shade and stick with it. (insert widely opened eyes and blank stare) God is not the author of confusion! (insert chuckling under her breath as she turns the page of the Sanctified Holy Ghost-filled Fire Baptized Traditional Christian Woman Attire Magazine). Nope, not that one. I wore that two years ago. No repeats in Jesus Name. The Bible says behold I do a new thing. Huh!! It's springing forth. Huh!! (insert raised handshake and sanctified facial expression). How you gon' be the pastor's wife and you lookin' like...(insert head shake of disagreement). That's why your fast-tail daughter...NO! (she quickly stands up and swipes her hands to signify an end to the commentary) Not today, Satan! We are not doing this today.

[Auntie takes a deep breath in and out to calm her nerves.] Good job, girl!!! You cut that devil off at the pass. [Auntie sits to signify the passing of her 'moment,' picks up the magazine and continues searching for convention attire.] You know what, let me get white. I need to show forth the purity of the Lord. These young women need to see the older women looking like what God said. Huh! That's right. Holiness is still right. Righteousness exalts a nation! Come on here church!!! Whew! Slow down girl. Save that for your Women's Day message. [Turning the pages] Let me look back here to see if they have the handkerchiefs to match these suits. [Before she could reach that area, she passed the 'foundation' section and saw a girdle she wanted to purchase. Slowing down to read the description, she begins a dialogue with herself.] Oh, look here. Firmly holds...silhouette...protection...moisture barrier. Alright now! That's it right there. It ain't right to jiggle in the house of the Lord. Got to hold all this goodness in place until the man of God comes. Although, girl you know you done got a lil loose here these days. Gotta tighten up this ship. We up a whole dress size since... (insert closed eyes and a raised finger to signify a halt to the dialogue. Tears begin to well up in her eyes.) No, no, no! Not today. We have done well today. I did my morning devotion, I called Mother Turner to pray with her before she went to surgery. I wrote out these 'Thank You' cards for the Women's Ministry, I did my noon day prayer call. I cleaned up 'round here, and I'm about to order my suit for convention. Now, I am separated for a greater work to do now that I'm single again. I am committed to the work of the Lord. [Wiping her eyes, she catches a glimpse of the clock.] Lord have Mercy! It's 8 o'clock. Let me take my blood pressure medicine and my insulin and get ready to watch my show. I'll wait thirty minutes and then have my piece of pound cake and ice cream. There ain't nothing wrong with a lil sweet every now and then, especially when you not married. Look here now! You gotta have some kinda pleasure in life. [Grunting and maneuvering to get up from the couch, Auntie encourages herself.] Come on girl. Get on up. We gotta get our stuff laid out for Bible Study tomorrow.

LET'S TALK ABOUT IT

Many, as it was for me and several others who come from an impoverished background, see their ability to "eat what I want" as a sign of prosperity. Let's have a truth moment:

How many of us have seen the mother in the store on the first of the month with a basket or two piled high with food? As you survey the basket and view box after box of snack cakes, bags of chips, bottles of soda, cartons of ice cream, and every other novelty food item you can think of, you think to yourself, "That don't make no sense! If she bought real food, it'll last 'til the end of the month!"

Can we be honest and say that we've had this thought at least once in our lifetime? I submit to you that the mother is not ignorant of the idea of what "real" food is. She, like many of us after having suffered lack in an area, look for an opportunity to fill that void. She, like many of us have, seized the opportunity to "stock up" on what she felt she missed out on; unfortunately to excess. Those of us who have lived through periods of poverty where we had no choice but to eat the same thing over and over have walked several miles in the shoes of this mother. Others, perhaps, never suffered lack in that way. Some come from families that had provision and overindulged as a matter of right. This family takes on the attitude of King Solomon in Ecclesiastes where he discusses how he withheld nothing from himself and experienced every pleasure possible. May I submit to you that the overindulgent person, though they have provision, is also impoverished? We learned in the last chapter about filling voids in the soul with consumption. This consumption can manifest in consumption and overindulgence in any area, but for the sake of this commentary, we will remain focused on food.

Poverty has a mindset, a narrative, a viewpoint that devalues what is common amongst it, i.e. I devalue what I have access to on a daily basis because it is readily available to me. Though instant noodles and canned pasta are low in nutritional value and have a host of preservatives and health-diminishing ingredients, it is food and will fill your belly for a moment in time. As a child I coveted these types of food. My mother home-cooked our breakfast, lunch, and dinner; even our snacks and treats at times. Children in our neighborhood seemed to show up at our house when my mother was making popcorn. We rarely had pre-prepared food items. At the time, because of my poverty mindset, I saw this as a deficit in my life experience and longed for what I saw my peers eating. Today, I look back and I see it as a sign of wealth. Very few of my peers had home cooked meals on a daily basis.

With the rise and popularity of convenience and microwaveable foods, many were leaving the practice of home cooking for special occasions. The convenience era, in my opinion, contributed to an increase in and prolonged occupation of poverty in many communities. Convenience costs! You can pay three to five times more for a smaller quantity of a product that is pre-prepared by means of hot food prep, canned, frozen, or freeze dried. If a box of pasta is $.89, a jar of sauce is $1.50, and Italian seasoning is $.98 and these ingredients will provide food for me for several days or a meal for my whole family, why in the world would I pay the same amount for a single serving of a food item?!?!?!? Convenience, another aspect of the poverty mentality says, "Give it to me now! I don't want to wait for it."

We must understand that poverty is a spirit (Matthew 5:3). And those who have suffered beneath its oppression are increasingly susceptible to overindulgence. The amplified version of this text explains that the person with a poverty mindset regards themselves as insignificant. This denotes the care taken of the body. When you value a thing, you take great care of it; this includes what you put into it. However, we must mature in our mindset to understand that our body is a vessel to be used for the Glory of God; the care we take of it denotes the value we see in it.

In the case of a mother regarding her children, most parents don't want their children to suffer through the struggles that they have faced. So, when we see the mother with the basket full of 'junk food' we must take a step back and understand her perspective. I have been in the position where I thought to myself, "When I get money, I'll eat what I want!" And, as a mother, she wants to see her children enjoy the foods that other children have the ability to purchase and have access to on a regular basis. She knows that it won't last but the point is that she has access to it now.

For many people, they view their ability to eat what they want as a sign of prosperity. Poverty mindset teaches us that lack or deprivation of a thing equals poverty. To have something withheld from you means that you cannot afford to have it. What if we viewed the denial of a thing as a safety precaution? We place our children inside a playpen to keep them safe from items and scenarios that can harm them. The playpen is a type of border, barrier, prevention that the child sees as an impediment to their freedom, but the adult KNOWS that the barrier is a protection from danger. As we mature in our faith and knowledge of God, we begin to understand the meaning of 1 Corinthians 10:23 NLT:

> "You say, 'I am allowed to do anything'—but not everything is good for you. You say, 'I am allowed to do anything'—but not everything is beneficial."

In other words, just because I CAN doesn't mean I SHOULD.

Some prefer the complacency and convenience of bondage to the process of Freedom. They desire the tastes of persecution to the fresh and nutrient-dense food of the Glory of God. The children of Israel complained about eating a miracle every day - manna. They complained about portion sizes. They complained about everything! They didn't see the value in God calling them out of bondage because they felt as though freedom would allow them to satisfy their appetites at will instead of it calling them into order. Owning a car gives you freedom, but there is maintenance and upkeep that must occur to maintain that vehicle and freedom. If you don't put gas in the car, change the oil, rotate the tires, and switch out the fluids, your newfound freedom will do you no good because it will be on the side of the road or sitting on bricks in your driveway. With Freedom comes new responsibilities and requirements, all for your benefit and the Glory of God. The Israelites were blinded by their appetites and couldn't see how the miraculous was their portion. They did not get sick, their clothes nor shoes bore holes, and they had strength daily to journey and follow the presence of God while carrying EVERYTHING they owned. They only did this by eating the provisionary food of the Father. He had a dietary construct for them to follow that benefited their overall life.

We also see in the books of Daniel and Esther how Abba has chosen some to be set apart and their obedience to that construct contributes to their health, appearance, and favor with God and men. Their commitment to their lifestyle included a specific dietary construct. This construct excluded groupings of food items and drinks. This discipline was in place, accepted, and followed PRIOR to Daniel, his friends, and Esther being elevated to prominent positions of authority in the kingdoms they lived in. The book of Esther states that she had "special" food (Esther 2:10 NIV) and Daniel's construct was very specific (Daniel 1:12). Each of them made commitments and walked out their difference in the company of those who were directly opposite of them. None of their peers operated on that level. What they consumed was a part of their preparation for prominence. These positions were not just a title or rank, but wealth came alongside it. Daniel and Esther both gained the favor of those who governed them. They both became known for their differences. Both were seen and recognized as attractive, and more so than their counterparts. Both ascended to positions of governance. And all after they obeyed the word of the Lord despite the attitudes and actions of the multitude in their company. Their difference made the difference between them and others.

If we shed our poverty mentality and view the parameters Abba has given us as a protection, preparation, and a propellant for the platform of our promised position of prominence, we would be postured for greatness.

Come, let's talk about why you think eating what you want = prosperity.

LET'S WORK THROUGH THIS TOGETHER

Prompts:

1. What does being set apart mean to you?

   _____
   _____
   _____
   _____

2. Describe your feelings in scenarios where you felt you were held to standards by God or man that seemed as though others in your life didn't have to meet?

   _____
   _____
   _____
   _____

3. Describe a moment in your past where you were like the mother in the grocery store.

   _____
   _____
   _____
   _____

4. What was your family's mindset toward the type of foods you ate? What narrative was common in your household regarding food?

___

5. Explain why you feel eating what you want = prosperity?

___

6. What commitment will you make TODAY to break the shackles of the poverty mindset over your family?

___

Encouragement:

Know this, if Abba has called you to a journey, He has graced you with the ability to complete it as He has designed. There is no account in scripture where God sent a person on a journey and did not provide for and equip them for it. At times, He explained before the journey was initiated and other times, He designated a person to meet them along the way to their destination. The fact is that Abba is so gracious and so loving that He will not leave us or forsake us. Rest in the assurance of knowing that He will meet you at EVERY crossroad with your next set of instructions, tools, elevated mindset, and methodology to reach the next threshold of your life. Don't be afraid of the journey...Difference makes the Difference.

Prayer:

Abba,

Thank you for loving me so much that you have called me to walk a road of distinction. There is a difference between those who are called by and covered under your name and those who are not. I recognize that being set apart is not a life of deprivation, but one of outpouring, grace, and supply. As your word teaches us, you exchange beauty for ashes and joy for sorrow. So, too, have you exchanged my former lifestyle for one that will bring me to greater prosperity and resource in your kingdom. I stand in agreement with your plan for my life.

In Jesus Name, it is so.

Amen

Open the Eyes of Your Heart

My Body: The Living Sacrifice

Scenario: It's two days later and Tonya continues her binge after being dropped by Auntie in a time of need. Tonya has gone to work and operated as she normally does but is now in a state of functional depression. Instead of coming home to sit in a dark room and cry, she is distracting her mind with food and entertainment.

Tonya begins to malign herself into a self-loathing posture to justify her extended binge. As she prepares her altar (the couch), she rehearses her list of sacrifices she has to offer and is preparing for her evening of desperately seeking stimulation.

[Tonya walks in exhausted from a day of pretending to be happy and plops down on the couch. She is physically drained but becomes energized by the thought of continuing her evening ritual of eating and entertaining herself to sleep so she doesn't have to face her recent emotional trauma. She picked up her arsenal of snacks on the way home and is ready to begin.]

(She prepares her coffee table and couch with pillows, blankets, napkins, drinks, and utensils for her buffet.) "Oh yes, honey! It's Thursday...Law & Order SVU marathon is tonight on USA." (She pauses her preparation to lift her hand in a witness and releases her tongues in praise.) "Somebody gotta get some justice 'round here." (insert facial expression: eyes wide open and rolling as she continues arranging her display of varied food items.) "But I feel like watching somebody get chopped in the back of they throat, in Jesus name. (Insert martial arts movements and an enthusiastic kick in the air.) "Kapiyow!!! Y'all ain't ready for me. I got that wig snatchin' anointing." (insert a Holy Ghost head shake and pious ugly holy face.) "I'll be done knocked somebody out 'round here and end up on death row. Sista be 'round here in a real-life episode of Orange is the New Black. Sis be on the chain gang. I'll be like Tupac ⊠Murder is the case that she gave me⊠ (Throwing up fake gang signs and doing her gangsta moves) (Eeking out a half-hearted chuckle) "Yeah, for real tho..." (She steps back to survey her set up and assure she has everything within reach from the couch.) "Ok, so I got my wings and fries, I had a ice cream sandwich earlier, but I got my chocolate chip cookies, my strawberry soda, and my strawberry cheesecake for later." (clapping her hands in agreement with her finished preparation) "Good job! Now let me get my jammies on and turn this AC down." (exiting the room and returning in her worship attire) "Lord God, I thank ya for whoever created bras for they minister unto my lady parts. But, MY GOD, I'm so glad to be set free when I come home. (insert a holy dance and tongues) I just wanna be free, Jesus. Yeeeesss Lord, I just wanna be free." (She quickly comes out of 'the spirit', standing over her spread and surveying the table she realizes something) "Ok, so let me make sure I got everything 'cause I don't wanna get up once I sit down." (Whispering to herself and repeating her menu she realizes the missing piece.) "Oh...yes Lord...I need that good hot sauce ministry, Amen?!?!?" (She hurries off to the kitchen and returns to the couch with the hot sauce.) [Arranging her pillows, covering up with her blanket, and settling into her well-worn groove in the couch, she grabs the plate of wings and fries and puts it in her lap. She blesses the food and begins eating.] "Ok, so we gon' start out with a couple episodes of SVU then we can get that good Jason Stathum in. Yaaassss...I gots to see my BooThang blow somebody up in Jesus Name. Bad guy gon' die today...they gon' learn today."

[It's now 6:30 a.m. the following morning and we find Tonya in the same position on the couch. She ate all ten wings and fries, half the bag of chocolate chip cookies, the cheesecake with the strawberry topping, drank the soda, and also had a dollar bag of chips with lemonade around midnight. Tonya frantically jumps up at the sound of her alarm after the third snooze.]

"Oh Lord!!! What ti-... (looking at her phone and realizing she is late). Je-sus fix it!!! I gotta be at a training at 7 a.m. downtown!" [Hurrying off the couch and into the bathroom to rinse her mouth with mouthwash, she begins to attempt to style her hair while she gargles. She spits and then sees herself in the mirror and takes a long pause.] "Tonya...you gotta stop doin' this. You always late! Need to carry your behind to sleep at night and stop eatin!!! You need to live right. It don't make no sense! You keep doin' the same thing over and over. I'm tired of this. Uuuuuggh! Ok, I'm so glad we wear a uniform. Don't nobody have to know it's the same one from yesterday." (While spraying an excessive amount of body spray to mask the fact that she hasn't showered the last three days, she grabs her bags and hurries toward the

> door.) "Ok, ok, ok! I'll just tell my supervisor my stomach was upset. I really don't feel good anyway." (Holding her stomach, she begins to rehearse her symptoms to herself and how bad she has been feeling.) Yeah, I do feel a lil warm and I don't know if this is heartburn or something more serious. I need to go back to the doctor. Maybe she can prescribe me something." (While closing up her apartment and locking the door she reflects on her life.) "Something ain't right. I need to do something about this."

LET'S TALK ABOUT IT

Roman's 12:1 says,

> "And so, dear brothers and sisters, I plead with you to give your bodies to God because of all he has done for you. Let them be a living and holy sacrifice—the kind he will find acceptable. This is truly the way to worship him. *(NLT)*

In the above scenario we see that Tonya has progressed into a destructive pattern after not receiving the response she felt her need deserved. This downward spiral into depression called up her addictive behaviors and amplified them into a marathon of idolatry. Not only did she continue to offer sacrifices of her time, attention, desires, and identity, but ALL these methods of self-abuse resulted in her body taking on damage. She recognized that she was not well but began to invite infirmity into her body to justify her choices and mask her depression from those in close proximity. Not only is her physical body being damaged by the overload of sugar, salt, and the plethora of preservatives in her food choices, but she has not bathed in the past three days! She continues to pile on artificial fragrances mixed with alcohol, dyes, and propellants to her skin and clothing to mask the odor of her desperation. The body requires cleansing to maintain its health. The best defense against illness is to wash your hands and keep away from sick people...but what happens if you are the sick person? What happens if you are the diseased vessel? How do you prevent that?

Addiction is a form of worship? Whatever has first place in your life is your god. We see that Tonya took great care to make preparation for her extensive food worship. Though these preparations took place outwardly, they started in her heart. The Bible teaches us that we are not to make plans to be fleshly (Romans 13:14). Desires, cravings, and addictions are physical manifestations of ties and bondages that have taken place in the soul. They indicate voids in the soul that are crying out to be filled. There are times when we crave certain foods as a sign that we are deficient in a nutrient. However, when the soul is as cluttered and bound as we see Tonya's is, we must first look to the spiritual, and not the natural.

Our Spirit is the highest form of our created being. It is the portion of us that is in sync with God and tuned to His frequency. Our Spirit communicates perfectly with the Father but if it has been silenced, drowned out, or ignored for an extended period of time, its voice will become dormant. The voice of our Spirit remains intact, but our refusal to heed the dialogue from the heavenly realm indicates to the Spirit that it is not welcomed to speak and operate in our lives as Abba designed it to.

No demand = No supply

How many of us would cease from speaking if each time we attempted to lift our voice we were silenced? God doesn't force us to hear Him. He speaks and we must choose to follow. Hebrews 3:15 says:

> "As it is said: Today, if you hear His voice, do not harden your hearts as in the rebellion." *(HCSB)*

"Today" indicates that Abba is always speaking and has a word ready for us to hear DAILY. If we would settle our soul, calling our mind, will, and emotions into subjection, we would hear the voice of God clearly through our Spirit. Imagine how the past three days would have been different for Tonya if she yielded her desire for the words of man and sought the voice of God. She erected an altar in her heart to her idol and sunk deeper into despair when the idols couldn't satisfy what she hungers and thirsts for.

An altar is a designated place you go to for worship through sacrifice. It is sacred, holy, special, significant. It is a distinct location that signifies and commands gifts. The couch in Tonya's living room became her physical altar. She regularly gathered there to offer up sacrifices to her gods: food, lust, desire, anger, perversion, entertainment, etc. She is so devout in her worship that she has worn a groove in the couch from her continuous sitting.

Your heart is a perpetual altar and your body is the ready sacrifice that burns continually upon it. Resulting in an aroma that is either pleasing or vile in the nostrils of God. Jesus is described as the lamb slain before the foundation of the world (Rev 13:8). Following Christ's example, means we, too, must be sacrificed to bring forth freedom. We are to be crucified with Christ (Gal 2:20) meaning, as He gave up His will for the Father's (Luke 22:42), we must follow suit. In a time of great distress and concern, He forfeited His desires and surrendered to the will of the Father. This is the essence of what it means to be a living sacrifice. Jesus could have chosen to exercise His power and authority at that moment. He could have commanded legions of Angels to remove Him from the situation, but in the heat of the moment He submitted to the perfect will and plan of our Father. What if He said no, I don't want to be a sacrifice? Calvary would not have happened which means our sins would not have been forgiven, and we would all be lost and destined for hell still cursed by the sin of the original man, Adam. Do you see how significant a YES is?

Take a moment and think of yourself, your body, as a sacrifice that purchases the freedom of GENERATIONS of your family. What if the decisions you make today ransoms your bloodline from the bondage of high blood pressure, diabetes, stroke, heart disease, and every other kind of physical infirmity? What if your "Yes, Lord!" breaks the chains of depression, schizophrenia, autism, or bipolar disorder? What if you realized that what you put into your body determines its efficiency, health, endurance, aesthetics, and fitness? It's not about your choice being taken away; it's about you making better choices. Our lifestyle breeds results. These results are desirable or not, but they are real. We must CHOOSE to be the sacrifice! Abba will not force us. He presents the opportunity and once we accept, He downloads the blueprint.

LET'S WORK THROUGH THIS TOGETHER

Prompts:

1. What do you think a sacrificial life looks like? Describe it in detail.

   _____
   _____
   _____
   _____

2. Identify the altars you feel are erected in your heart? Name them below.

   _____
   _____
   _____
   _____

3. Describe a situation where you responded as Tonya did above. What was the trigger that initiated the situation? After reading this chapter, how would you change your response?

   _____
   _____
   _____
   _____

4. What do you feel prevents you from giving God your YES?

_____
_____
_____
_____

Encouragement:

Romans 8:1 says, "There is therefore now no condemnation to them which are in Christ Jesus, who walk not after the flesh, but after the Spirit." (KJV). No matter how far you have sunk into the pits of life, you have never gone too far that Abba can't reach you. No matter how many weeks, months, years, or decades you have lived outside the will of God, there is still hope. Don't talk yourself out of freedom. You can be free from every chain and fetter. Every bondage can be broken…it already has been. When Jesus died for our sins He rose with ALL power in His hands. He holds the keys to death, hell, and the grave. The key to your freedom is to surrender. Be the sacrifice. Value the vessel Abba will use to bring forth your DESTINY. How can you walk in the inheritance He desires for you if your body is broken down, diseased, and damaged from the decisions you've made to sacrifice your being to idols that NEVER had the capacity to fulfill your needs?

It's not too late. Choose today! Who will you serve? God or self, God or man, God or desire. He has a place and a plan for you. All that's needed is a YES...Yes to the will of God, Yes to the plans of God, Yes to the purpose of God. Yes to surrender...YES to being the sacrifice.

Prayer:

Abba,

You know my name. You know my innermost parts. You know all my needs, wants, and desires. You know what plagues my mind and torments my soul. Thank you for being a Deliverer. Thank you for providing a way of escape. Thank you for having already won the victory for me. You set me free on Calvary, and I take hold of that freedom. Today I choose FREEDOM through surrender. I offer myself as a willing sacrifice on your altar. I knock down every altar in my heart, and I erect a single altar for you. I position myself upon it and die to my old life. Thank you that TODAY I am made new in Christ. I go forward into my future a new creature surrendered to your will.

It is so, in Jesus Name
Amen

Cleansing: Set your affections on things above

Scenario: It's now 11a.m. on Friday. Tonya recognized this morning that she needs to make some changes after spending the past three days binging on food and entertainment to the neglect of her personal hygiene. She is now at work plagued by thoughts of Krispy Kreme donuts. Tonya used to go there as a treat with Auntie when she was a little girl while her mom was working. She has been thinking about going there since she got a text alert and email at 8am with a 20% off coupon. She is all about saving money since she has spent quite a bit on her recent binge. Thankfully the training has concluded, and she got a call from a client that lives on that side of town requesting a resource. Tonya rushes through completing a task and gathering her materials for her visit so she can make it to the lobby by noon when the "Hot" light comes on.

[Tonya is in the car driving to the Krispy Kreme when she gets a call] (Ring Ring)

Tonya: Hello, this is T-

Client: Ms. Tonya, I'm not home no more. I had to run out real quick.

Tonya: Gurl! Imma whoop you! I'm already halfway there.

Client: I'm sorry Ms. Tonya. My momma had to go do something and she needed my car.

Tonya: How long before you get back?

Client: Maybe a hour.

Tonya: OK, I'll stay on this side of town for a lil bit. If you don't text me by 1pm you will have to reschedule.

Client: Ok, Ms. Tonya, Imma call you. (call ends and Tonya tosses the phone onto her passenger seat)

[Rolling her eyes and huffing, she begins her commentary of excuses to justify her trip to the donut shop.] Child Boo! She not gon' call back. Anyway, that'll just give me a lil time to get my mind right. This why I need doggone donuts! (insert aggressive hand gestures and hits on the steering wheel) 'Cause folk don't wanna live right! (insert widely opened eyes with the angry Momma face.) See, Jesus knew folk was gon' work my nerve today, that's why He blessed me with this coupon. Praise Him! Bless the name of the Lord. Hah!!! Praise Him with the timbrel and dance. (insert a holy head shake and waving hand in praise.)

[Pulling into the parking lot, Tonya lifts up tongues of praise and quickens when she sees she has beat the crowd.]

(While choosing her parking space, she notices a familiar car in the lot.) Oh heck to the No!!! Why is Auntie in here? Don't she have some Bingo to play or somethin' to sew? (Rolling her eyes and huffing, she makes a decision.) Whatever! It is what it is. I already called my order in and I'll just act like I don't see her, get my two donuts, and leave. I'm only gettin' two 'cause I'm trying to live right! I ain't got time for her no way. She ain't called me back all week. (insert teeth sucking noise as she exits and secures her vehicle)

[Tonya has no idea that Auntie has watched her have her temper tantrum and determines that she will not allow a "lil gurl" to ignore her. Since she helped raise her, she knows her responses and all the right buttons to push.] (Tonya enters and goes directly to the cashier looking straight ahead, pretending not to see Auntie sitting at the table to the right. While trying to remain aloof, she hears this exaggerated greeting.)

Auntie: Well, hello lil gurl! I said hello lil gurl (smirking with pleasure at her successful mission to disrupt Tonya's attempt to ignore her while she stares at the menu and fidgets while desperately striving to ignore the person who triggered her recent binge.)

Tonya: (Finally relenting, Tonya drops her head with closed eyes to gain her composure and calm her nerves; she puts a halfhearted smile on her face and turns to engage the conversation.) Hello! How are you?

Auntie: (in her sarcasm saturated tone with matching facial expression) Oh, I'm excellent! Headed to my sewing circle for our monthly meeting.

Tonya: (Tonya quickly turns back toward the line and bellows a laugh toward the ceiling) Ha!!! Lord help today. (regaining her poise and adjusting the smirk on her face, she turns back toward Auntie fighting back further outbursts.) So, how have you been?

Auntie: (Now upset to see she no longer had control of the situation, Auntie takes the opportunity to be nice-nasty and politely insult Tonya with a sarcastic tone.) Oh honey, them folks must be working you too hard down there. You need to make sure you come up to my church on Saturday. We havin' a deliverance meeting. You need to get that devil out, sweetheart!

Tonya: Oh, on the contrary. I'm excellent! But it's a good thing that you'll be in the atmosphere since you're ordering your usual two dozen for the weekend. (Tonya is now smiling with a look of 'check mate' on her face. You see, Tonya knows Auntie as well and grew up eating two dozen donuts WITH her every weekend).

Auntie: (With an angry look, a tightly curled lip, rolling eyes, and rage bubbling up from her heart to her mouth, Auntie responds very sharply.) Lil gurl, I told you I was going to my sewing circle. I'm not gone eat all them donuts by myself.

Tonya: Right! That's why you in a size what now? [still standing in line facing the front she turns slightly to the right and gives Auntie a 'side eye' waiting for a response she knows she'll never get. Pleased with having beaten Auntie at her own game she resumes her original posture with a grand smile on her face and continues waiting for her order. Her victory is made evident by Auntie's lowered head and silence] (Hearing her name called, with sarcasm and guile oozing through her body language, she enthusiastically goes up to retrieve it.) Exactly…uuummm that's my order. Let me get my two donuts and go on my way… (Blowing a kiss, smiling, waving, and exiting the building she gives her final comment.) You have a blessed day, Auntie. Sew well.

[Auntie sits motionless at the table waiting for her donut order to be filled in silence. She is angry, hurt, embarrassed, and in disbelief that she was publicly outed by Tonya, that she had no rebuttal because her comments were true, and that she was beaten at her game by the one she taught it to… the game of manipulation and control by emotional warfare]

[Filled with the joy of her recent victory, Tonya inhales her two donuts before she can exit the parking lot. Feeling the sugar hit her blood stream she has a great idea.] Since I'm already over here, let me go ahead and see what Ross has in there. I'll just walk around and look. I'll leave my wallet in the car so I don't buy nothin', unless it's on clearance. If I leave it there, they won't have it when I come back. (Tonya pulls off still reeling by what just took place and the massive sugar rush from the glazed donuts.)

[Hearing Tonya's car crank up; Auntie finally lifts her head. She knows it's safe, and she won't have to look Tonya in the eye. She watches Tonya pull off as tears fall from her eyes. She realizes that she taught Tonya to behave that way but never thought it would come back to bite her. Hearing her name called, she goes up to receive her order. As soon as she gets settled in the car, she opens the box and begins to eat before she cranks her vehicle.]

(Arriving home, having ridden in silence Auntie looks down and realizes that she has eaten ten of the twelve donuts without thinking. Auntie exclaims) Lord have mercy!!! What happened to my donuts?!?!?!?

LET'S TALK ABOUT IT

Here we see Tonya and Auntie both perverting the use of food. Some may think that perversion is a harsh word to be used here but we must understand that perversion is misuse of a thing. To use something out of context, beyond the purpose it was created and intended for, means that you have perverted it. The Holman Illustrated Bible Dictionary (Draper & Brand, 2003) states that people, speech, mindsets, and ways can be perverse. Tonya and Auntie both perverted the use of food by creating excuses that enabled them to continue in long standing patterns of behavior. Tonya grew up binge eating with Auntie on the weekends and we see that she has continued the practice. So, we can conclude that the perverse view of food is generational. Philippians 2:15 and Deuteronomy 32:5 teach us that an entire generation of people can be perverse. Our families are part of these generations. Look at your family and explore patterns of behavior...what similarities do you see from your parents, grandparents, great grandparents, and beyond?

Did you know that you can inherit more than physical attributes from your family? Learned behaviors can and should be seen as an inheritance. By sitting on the couch binge eating sweets and watching television as a child, Tonya learned to view food and entertainment as 'fun,' 'comfort,' a method of self-care, and relaxation. She also learned how to create the excuses that give her 'permission' to continue. Tonya even goes so far as to pervert the praise and provision of God by attributing the receipt of the coupon to purchase donuts as a blessing. The truth is that she downloaded that app to feed her addiction. The coupon is a marketing ploy to provoke those who would otherwise not make a purchase to do so. She was bound to receive a coupon or advertisement at some point. The provision of God will never lend itself to perversion of any kind. Addiction is a trap and the grace and provision of God will never lead you to bondage.

Tonya quickly transitioned from recognition of fault in her behavior pattern to altering her work schedule to satisfy her intense desire for a donut. Not to mention her perversion of the truth to insult Auntie. Her statements were true, but the intent of her heart was malicious. This does not please God. Especially when she was in the same location, buying the same food, for the same reason… addiction. Yes, she purchased a lesser amount, but the fact is that she was there for the same reason. We misrepresent (pervert) the heart of God and others' view of Him when we assign degrees and hierarchy to sins. Romans 3:23 tells us that everyone sins and falls short. Some use this verse to justify continuing in sin. However, Romans 6:1 makes it clear that we should not continually sin. Instead, we should recognize our error, repent, turn away from the practice of sin, and seek God for wisdom on how not to end up in that place again.

We can be in a pattern of behavior for so long that we don't realize our actions. Auntie drove all the way home blindly eating. She was so consumed by her emotions that she didn't recognize her level of consumption. How many of us have sat to complete a task with a snack and before you know it you have hit the bottom of the bag and had no idea when or how you ate it so fast? I've been there and done that too many times to count.

We must come to the place where we desire the pureness of all of God's creation. In order to be free from the bondages that plague our hearts, minds, and emotions (the Soul) we must seek the purity of God. We must allow the cleansing and purifying water of God to purify our mind. Can you imagine how the scenario would have been different if Tonya had immediately brought her thoughts into subjection? She sat for hours thinking about donuts before she finally gave in and devised a plan to fulfill her desire.

> Romans 13:14 says, "But put on the Lord Jesus Christ, and make no provision for the flesh, to gratify its desires." *(ESV)*

Colossians 3:2 says, "Set your mind on the things that are above, not on the things that are on the Earth." *(WEB)*

Isaiah 26:3 says, "You will keep the mind that is dependent on You in perfect peace, for it is trusting in You." *(HCSB)*

Joshua 1:8 says, "Study this Book of instruction continually. Meditate on it day and night so you will be sure to obey everything written in it. Only then will you prosper and succeed in all you do." *(NLT)*

Philippians 4:8 says, "And now, dear brothers and sisters, one final thing. Fix your thoughts on what is true, and honorable, and right, and pure, and lovely, and admirable. Think about things that are excellent and worthy of praise." *(NLT)*

These scriptures make it clear that what we think about should be the things that will please God. We can also deduce from these texts that the mind is a gateway to our heart. Whatever we meditate on will germinate in our heart and grow to become a vineyard that the vine dresser

(John 15:1-17) is welcomed and desires to visit. OR we can become a wilderness overgrown with weeds, thorns, and thistles. Just as we chastise and discipline our children when we see behaviors and patterns that we know will lead them toward harm, so too must we chastise our minds. We must bring it into complete subjection to the perfect will of God.

Inordinate (perverse) affections put our minds on a path toward harm. When we make hurt, wounds, deficits, and desires our meditation, we end up on a collision course toward prolonged addiction, stronger bondage, and deeper voids in the soul. In order to devise effective strategies for freedom, we must first become a student of our current and past state of mind and being.

Come with me as we dissect and study the above scenario.

LET'S WORK THROUGH THIS TOGETHER

Prompts:

1. How many perversions can you identify in Tonya and Auntie's exchange besides food? List them below. Explain why you feel this is a perversion.

   _____
   _____
   _____
   _____

2. What other inherited behaviors did you notice? Explain why these behaviors are perverse?

   _____
   _____
   _____
   _____

3. How have you been perverse in your view of food? Are these learned behaviors from childhood, or did you pick them up later in life?

   _____
   _____
   _____
   _____

4. How did their emotions support their perversion?

   _____
   _____
   _____
   _____

5. What inherited behaviors do you recognize in your life? List below.

   _____
   _____
   _____
   _____

6. How do the behaviors of your extended family members expose the perversion of your forefathers?

   _____
   _____
   _____
   _____

Encouragement:

Don't be dismayed. I lived decades of my life mimicking the cycles we see in Tonya and Auntie before I realized that I could be free. I did not understand that my meditation on a person, place, or thing and its effects on me was reinforcing my bondage. I had no idea that my rituals surrounding 'self-care', fun, and relaxation were ensnaring my mind. I just didn't know.

But, be encouraged! All is not lost. There is hope and help for change in this area. There are several scriptures listed above that you can use as a weapon against the flood of perverse thoughts and behaviors from the enemy. Luke 4:9-13 and Matthew 4:1-11 recount how Jesus overcame the temptation of the enemy by quoting scripture. When the enemy came, His response was, "It is written..." EVERY SINGLE TIME!!!! You need to know that you cannot reason with, negotiate, or bribe your way out of bondage. The only sure-fire weapon to defeat the enemy *is* the word of God. When the enemy comes with floods of perversion, raise the standard of the word of God. Stand in Faith agreement with it and remain steadfast.

It IS possible...you CAN, you WILL, and you MUST overcome.

Prayer:

Abba,

Thank you for loving me so much that you gave your only begotten son to save me. He is our high priest that can identify with everything that comes against our soul. He took on a human body to experience everything that comes against the existence of man. This makes Him a perfect intercessor for all of creation. I thank you that your word is true, sure, and sharp. Jesus is the Living Word, the word made flesh. I thank you that in times of struggle I can lift the name of Jesus and the flood of the enemy will cease. Thank you for giving me the victory in this battle.

In Jesus name I declare that my name is Victory. In Jesus name I decree and declare that I am victorious in every battle. My victory was won at Calvary and I walk in it.

It is so in Jesus name, Amen

Discipline

Scenario: [It's 8 p.m. on Friday and Auntie is sitting on the couch watching her 'stories.' She not only finished the first dozen donuts but is two-deep into the second dozen. She never made it to her sewing circle, hasn't taken her diabetes medication, and did not go for her evening walk. She has been in her housecoat and firmly planted on the couch since she got home from the donut shop.]

(While intently watching her show, she reaches into the box to grab another donut while exclaiming to the TV, with gestures, at the appalling behaviors of the characters. Smacking and 'blessing out' the villain of the show, Auntie answers a call from her sister who is watching the same program)

Auntie: "Hello! Girl yes!! I wish that rascal was right here. I'd slap fire outta him and drop my leg cross her chest in Jesus Name! (Slapping her leg and shaking her head side to side she exclaims) She can't do nothin' with this ham hock thunda thigh!! All her breath be gone! Raggedy tails know good and well they wrong."

Sister: "Sho ya right!!! Look here! A whole beat down in Jesus Name. Raggedy tails is right!"

Auntie: "Chiiillleeee, I know it! I'd be on death row fo sho! Clink clink (insert hand gestures that mimic hand cuffs) ...hear me?!?!"

Sister: "What ARE you eating? You smackin' like ten thousand dinosaurs in my ear. You sound like that TRex from Jurassic Park when he ate that goat. HAAAAAAA! You remember that?"

Auntie: "Girl it's just a donut. Tomorrow my cheat day but it's alright."

Sister: "A DONUT...Oh really??? You showin' out! How many have you had?"

Auntie: (trying to laugh off the rebuke of her sister) "Ha Ha Ha...Not that many. I still got some left."

Sister: "Nih you know good and well you ain't got NO business..."

Auntie: (cutting off her sister in mid-sentence to avoid the impending beratement) "Ok, ok, ok! Let me go on to the bathroom. I'll call you back later. Ok, bye."

"Alright now girl...you done ate too much. I don't know why you let that lil gurl get to you today. You wiped her butt and bought her shoes...mmhm. Disrespectful tail! That's ok, when I see her again it's gon' be on and poppin'. The Bible say touch not mine anointed and do my prophets no harm!!! That's what it say, mmhm. I don't know who she *thought* she was talking to but Imma handle her...believe that!!!" (Struggling to get up from the couch, Auntie sees the results of her emotional binge and decides that she needs to balance her sweets with a lil salt.) "Oh Chile! Let me get on to the bathroom and when I come back, I'll get me some chips to go with these donuts. All this sugar ain't good, girl. You need to balance this thang out with some saltiness. The Bible say a false balance is an abomination...mmhm...that's what it say!" (Passing through her bedroom on her way back from the bathroom, Auntie pulls the sour cream and onion potato chips from her nightstand and heads back to the living room couch. Returning to the same spot, Auntie plops down and grunts as she adjusts herself into a comfortable position).

(Auntie continues her commentary of self-encouragement as she opens her bag of chips) "Yes honey, we gots to do better. Can't be getting caught up with these lil raggedy children. It's ok tho...I will see her again. Anyway...let me get my show back on. Where my- aaahhh...ok." (sipping on her large cup of ice water she placed on the end table, Auntie continues) "Yes honey, I needs my water. Gotta keep this temple clean, Amand?!?!?" (lifting a shaking hand in agreement with herself and a quicken signified by the jerk of her whole body) "Alright now...gotta wash this all down in Jesus Name. I rebuke indigestion and heartburn. Oh yes! I'm going to sleep tonight in Jesus Name. Oh yes AND Amand! Glory to the most-high God."

[Auntie finishes the evening on the couch watching reruns of her favorite stories on demand and falls asleep after feasting on leftover fried chicken, mac 'n cheese, greens, yams, dressing, gravy, rice, black-eyed peas, and pineapple sweet tea she had left over from her dinner she prepared before Wednesday night Bible Study. Auntie spends most of Saturday napping on and off with a headache as her body attempts to process all the complex sugars, excessive salt, preservatives, chemicals, artificial flavors and colors, animal protein, fat, and complex carbs she ate all day Friday. We'll have to catch up with her later.]

[It's now 8 a.m. on Sunday and Tonya wakes and is staring at the ceiling contemplating how she can 'get out of' going to church. Tonya spent all day Saturday shopping and is exhausted. She had no junk food, didn't stop at 7Eleven® for any snacks, ate salad for lunch, and a Lean Cuisine® for dinner. She even showered Friday and Saturday night before binge watching Netflix. She has been in great spirits since her encounter with Auntie Friday afternoon.]

"I am tired! I don't feel like going nowhere. I been good. I haven't eaten any junk and I took my shower. I'm fresh and clean. I deserve a day to do what I want. Imma just watch TV church while I'm making my grits, eggs, corn beef hash, bacon, and toast. It's ok 'cause this my cheat day. I eat whatever I want on my cheat day...Amen?!?!? Oh Yes I do." (Insert a shaking head of agreement) I'm just gon' sit in here and watch service while I eat and then I'll clean up 'round here."

(Tonya fixed her nostalgic breakfast from childhood and yelps in agreement with a full mouth at the preacher.) "Oh yessuh!!! Praise Him, Bishop. Hoooooo! Won't He do it?!" (Tonya puts her plate down on the coffee table for a minute to give God praise with a dance.) "Hallelujah!!! Oh Yes God!" (Out of breath and chuckling to herself she gives herself wise counsel.) "Let me sat down before my neighbors call the office on me." (Resuming eating her breakfast, Tonya bellows a Hallelujah as the broadcast closes with a third praise break.) "HALLELUJAAAAAAHH!!! Whew chile! I know they tired. See, that's why I'm not there. I'm already tired."

(Returning to the couch after putting her plate in the sink, Tonya begins to find reasons NOT to do what SHE said she would.) "Chile, I'm tired and I ain't had no time to relax and just do me. I was out all day yesterday. I had to get my fit together for the party next weekend." (Turning the living room into a runway, Tonya demonstrates her model sashay entrance to the party.) "I gots to strut honey." (Snapping her fingers) "Yaaaassss! Matching head to toe! Not like Sis. Walters with all them shades of green on." (Closing her eyes and leaning her head back, Tonya bellows) "Ha!!! God can't be pleased with that mess. I know He ain't."

[Hearing her phone buzz, she sits on the couch and picks up to respond to who or whatever. "Tonya sees the time and realizes that she has spent a whole hour convincing herself NOT to do what SHE said and as she scrolls through social media,] "Oh Lord! It's 12 o'clock. Ok, in ten more minutes I'll get up and start cleaning up." (More time passes, and Tonya is prompted by a hunger pang to look at the clock.) "Oh Lord! It's 2 o'clock. Oh no ma'am, Ms. Tonya! Get your butt up. Let me make my lunch and get to cleaning." (Tonya goes to the kitchen to make her lunch and realizes she didn't go grocery shopping Saturday because she was getting her outfit ready. Tonya only has the other half of the pack of cookies she had Thursday night, half a gallon of lemonade, pork rinds, and some light bread.) "Dang girl!!! We on skid row huh?!?! Whatever! Ya girl know how to put some stuff together. Amen?!?! Let me see what's in this freezer." (Opening the freezer to find a frozen sausage link, she exclaims in thanksgiving) "Hallelujah to the most-high God. Now, normally I don't eat no swine but we gon' go 'head and partake today. I'm glad my Momma left this in here when she came the last time." (Tonya fixed her sausage sandwich and sets up her meal on the coffee table and gives herself instruction) "Ok girl. We gon' say grace, eat, and then clean up. Let me check my phone. It's been buzzing like crazy."

[It's now 7 p.m. and Tonya is asleep on the couch. She spent another hour and a half scrolling, posting, and responding to posts on social media, then fell asleep after consuming the whole bag of pork rinds, all the cookies, half of the link made into two sandwiches, and three quarters of the half gallon of lemonade. As she wakes up, she is surprised to see that it's dark outside.]

(Stretching and grunting) "Lord help today! What time is it?" (Continuing to stretch and feeling around on the couch for her phone, she finds it and exclaims) "Oh, uh uh! Not 7 o'clock...chile boo. Ain't nobody cleaning up today. I need to be relaxed so I can go back to work tomorrow. I gotta be right in the head to deal with these people. Let me get my lil happy tail up to this bathroom!

(Returning from the restroom) "Oohhh! I got heartburn...I don't know if it was them pork rinds, the hot sauce, or that sausage. See! That's why God said don't eat no pork!!! The skin part don't count 'cause that's not the meat but honey them chops and carrying on will getcha every time. Let me eat some bread to soak up this grease. Lord have mercy! My chest is burning" [Tonya returns to the couch with her four pieces of toast spread with butter and jelly. She spends the next hour flipping channels before deciding to watch her favorite movie for the umpteenth thousandth time.]

Can you see any familiar patterns of behavior in this scenario? Let's see what's really going on here.

LET'S TALK ABOU IT

Proverbs 11:1 says, "A false balance is an abomination to the LORD, but a just weight is his delight." (ESV). Auntie quoted a portion of this scripture but used it out of context. She used it to justify a poor choice and endorse her desire to continue her emotional eating binge. When studying this text in several versions of the Bible, I found that this scripture is related to business practices. This was very interesting to me because, as you may recall, I encouraged you to view your health as a part of your wealth, prosperity, and abundant life. Abba wants us to be integral in our dealings with ourselves and others. We can't achieve that standard if we are dishonest and out of order.

Auntie was not being a good steward of her bodily resource. She greatly compromised her asset by operating with a false balance. Eating more junk food from a different flavor profile does not balance a poor choice. I enjoy combinations of flavors and frequently encourage my clients to mix and match palettes to avoid ruts in their diet and promote creativity. However, sweet and savory do

NOT cancel one another. This is what Auntie was trying to portray with her misuse of the Word of God. She was perverted in her view of this text, and therefore perverted the word of God. That is a very dangerous practice. If we are honest with ourselves, there have been several times in our lives that we have manipulated the truth to meet our needs and fuel our desires. That is a false balance.

Verse 2 of Proverbs 11 says, "When pride comes, then comes disgrace, but with the humble is wisdom." (ESV). Pride is a very sneaky spirit. It hides itself in our mindsets, agendas, opinions, and decisions to do or not do a thing. When we justify our lusts with 'cheat days' and the continual delays of goal achievement, as we saw with Tonya, we are in essence putting our agenda and what we think, feel, and believe above that of the Father. That, ladies and gentlemen, is pride. To think or act in a manner that exalts your desire above the mandate of God is prideful and rebellious. Both are brought into subjection and eventually cast out by applying disciplines to your lifestyle that starve them to death. Every time we break ranks and go down our own path, we are 'feeding the monster.' We must think of our soul as prime real estate. 2 Corinthians 5:1 teaches us that our body is the *house* or dwelling place of our spirit. 1 Corinthians 6:19 explains that our body is the temple of the Holy Spirit. The temple, the appointed gathering place for worship, is described as the house of God in Ecclesiastes 5:1. We see in these texts that our body is a dwelling place. We make our homes comfortable and pleasing for our peace and joy...the enemy does the same in your soul. When permissions are granted through our actions, thoughts, mindsets, compromises, and decisions, we make our soul a plush pad for the enemy and his darkness to dwell. Every time we choose pleasure above purpose, we reinforce the bondages of our soul that affect our body, the ultimate asset to obtain and maintain wealth and prosperity.

The human body takes twenty-one to forty days to feel the effects of starvation (Silver, 2018) and forty-five to sixty-one days to die from it (Janiszewski, 2015). Since we were made in the image and likeness of God (Genesis 5:1) and He is a Spirit (John 4:24), we can deduce that the spiritual realm and the natural realm mirror one another. Therefore, if it takes a length of time for our natural body to starve to death, it will take a length of time for the spirits that take up residence in our soul to 'die'... and essentially make a decision that our body is no longer a habitable place to live. Our applied disciplines cut off their life source and produce an atmosphere in our 'house' that is not conducive for their continued habitation. Have you ever visited someone's home that was always cold or hot? You have difficulty in the environment, but they thrive because they have made the environment comfortable for them. This is what occurs in the spiritual/soulish realm. The spirits that dominate the real estate determines the conditions. If our disciplines starve them, we should be committed to constructs and processes that assist us to be free from their control and influence.

As I walked through my health journey, I committed myself to the processes Abba revealed to me step by step. My process of reverting back to the Garden Agenda looked like this:

First Transition	**Pescatarian** No land meat, only fish with scales	6 months
Second Transition	**Vegetarian** I ate pasta and other items that are made with animal products like breads, yogurt, cheese, etc.	3 months
Third Transition	**Veganism** I was plant-based with no meat, but there were a few items that Abba allowed me to consume until He led me to the choice He desired for me	1 month
Fourth Transition	**Complete Veganism** No animal products. Nothing made with an animal product as an ingredient	**Current Construct**

He revealed each step to me as I submitted, obeyed, and walked out His instructions. I have food allergies. While I am believing God for complete healing in that area, I must also be mindful of and guard myself against adverse effects. My Garden Agenda may seem stringent to some, but this is what I am called to for the optimal use and health of my temple. As you surrender to the disciplines Abba gives for your transition, He will lay out the intricacies tailor-made for your specific dietary construct.

Prior to these major shifts, Abba began to slowly reduce and eliminate the consumption of smaller obsessions. In the past I consumed lots of soda and sweet drinks. There was a process in place that helped me to reduce then eliminate soda and sugary drinks all together.

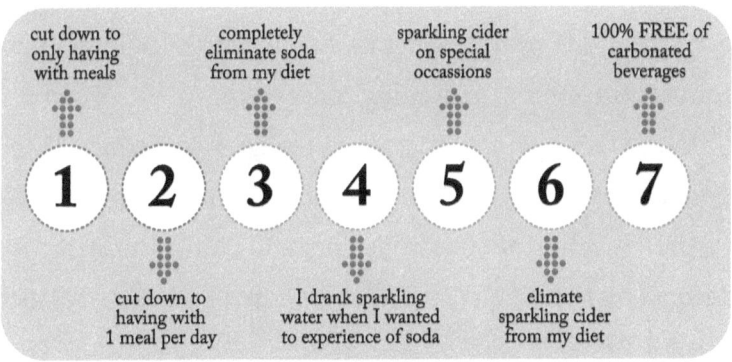

Today I praise God that it has been over five years since I have had a soda, two years since I drank lemonade, and one year since I had a glass of sweet tea. We ensure our success through obedience and the realistic expectation that change will not occur overnight. Many have tried and failed when trying to quit a habit, addiction, or destructive behavior. We must allow our bodies time to withdraw from the substance. Food addiction/dependency is the same as any other addiction. The severity differs from person to person but the principles surrounding the operation of that spirit are the same. We must understand that the spiritual realm has order and if we are to succeed in warring for our freedom, we must first line up with the order set forth at creation. When we bring our bodies into subjection, we begin to slowly but surely loosen the grip of the bondage that has ruled over and governed our soul. I believe in miracles, signs and wonders. Some have experienced an immediate deliverance from bondage in many different areas. However, let us be sure that we are not perverting the performance or solicitation of a miracle to subvert the *process* of coming to freedom.

Verse three of the same chapter goes on to say, "The integrity of the upright guides them, but the crookedness of the treacherous destroys them." (ESV). Integrity is defined by Merriam-Webster dictionary online (2020) as:

1. "Firm adherence to a code of especially moral or artistic values: INCORRUPTIBILITY
2. An unimpaired condition: SOUNDNESS
3. The quality or state of being complete or undivided: COMPLETENESS"

Integrity is a noun, meaning that it applies to a person, place, or thing. Therefore, every aspect of our life must have integrity. We must be integral in our speech, our actions, relationships, business practices, financial management, dietary construct, and how we represent and approach God's throne.

While this may seem harsh to some, for those who are desperately seeking FREEDOM, it is a small sacrifice for the reward of broken chains, released bondages, lifted weights of heavy burdens, and wicked kingdoms being torn down in our soul. Romans 8:19 expounds on the previous sentiment by reminding us that what we suffer now will later reveal the glory of God in us.

Will you choose to be glorious or will you remain in grave clothes?

LET'S WORK THROUGH THIS TOGETHER

Prompts:

1. What's the first sign you noticed that Auntie has no discipline with her eating habits? Did you notice anything in other chapters? Explain.

   _____
   _____
   _____
   _____

2. Explain why you feel Tonya was successful with not eating junk food, snacking, and attending to her personal hygiene.

   _____
   _____
   _____
   _____

3. What similarities did you notice in Auntie's and Tonya's binge a few chapters ago?

   _____
   _____
   _____
   _____

4. List the areas of life you feel Tonya needs to apply discipline. How many of these same areas do you feel you need to apply discipline? How do you think these areas relate to her eating habits?

_____
_____
_____
_____

5. What justifications did Tonya give for her behavior? Do you feel these are valid justifications? Describe a scenario where you have used these same excuses? Why did you feel they were valid in your situation?

_____
_____
_____
_____

6. How would you describe Auntie's response to her sister's rebuke? Do you feel her sister was wrong to address her behavior? Explain your answer.

_____
_____
_____
_____

7. Why do you think Sister gave that kind of response? What do you think is the motivation behind her berating Auntie?

_____
_____
_____
_____

8. Reflect on a situation where you were receiving a rebuke for your choices. Describe your feelings at that moment. Now, reflect on an instance where you were administering the rebuke to another person. How did the person respond to you? What was your motivation for addressing the person's behavior?

_____
_____
_____
_____

9. Describe what a disciplined lifestyle looks like to you.

_____
_____
_____
_____

Encouragement:

Beloved, be encouraged. Know that no matter the length of time that you have lived in disorder, chaos, malice, and reproach, there is yet time for you to REDEEM the time. Our Father (Abba) is the creator of all things (Elohim)... even time. He exists outside of time and can 'catch you up' to the exact place He desires you to be. I am a witness that He will do such a work in you that you won't recognize yourself.

When I first began going to the gym to work out, I saw people smirk and laugh at the chubby girl coming to join the gym. I didn't let the scoffs and disbelief of others deter me from fulfilling the call I KNOW Abba mandated for me. My obedience to His shift saved my natural and Spiritual life. Obedience is better than sacrifice. Will you be made whole? Will you accept the freedom that has already been bought and paid for by the finished work of the cross at Calvary? Make the decision TODAY!!! Decide to be disciplined.

Prayer

Abba,

I thank you so much for loving me past my fleshly desires and seeing me according to your original plan for my life. You created me for a purpose, and my physical body must be healthy to endure to the end of the race I've been called to. I submit this vessel to your perfect will, and I surrender to your call to discipline. Thank you for your grace and mercy. With you leading me, I will never fail.

In Jesus Name,
Amen

Fit For Battle: Armor On

Temptation

Scenario - It's now 8:45 p.m. on Sunday and Tonya is well into watching her favorite movie, quoting the lines, and mimicking the behaviors of the characters until she receives a text that changes everything.

[While watching the movie, Tonya gets a text from her long-lost boyfriend. She has been so busy shopping, eating, and entertaining herself that she forgot that she hasn't heard from him *all* week...even after she texted him from work regarding her crisis.]

(Hearing her phone buzz and chime, Tonya responds.) Who is this and why are they bothering me while I'm watching my-? Ooooohhh, Hey Boo! Oh, unht un! I ain't heard from your raggedy tail all week? What you want?

(Reading the text, tears begin to well up in her eyes) Text Says: Hey Tonya, I know we haven't talked all week. I needed some time to think. I need some space. I've been thinking about life and how I see myself in the future and to be honest, I don't see you there. There are certain traits I'm looking for in a wife and I just don't see those in you, not now anyway. I think the best thing for me to do is to leave this situation alone. There's nothing wrong with you, I think you're great, but I just don't see you as my wife. I don't wanna hold you or me up for the right person. I wish you the best. (Tonya puts the phone down, pauses the movie and sits on the couch in silence with tears streaming down her face.)

[It's 10pm Sunday and Tonya has no more tears to cry. She went through her phone several times trying to decide who to call to pour her heart out to but found no one who she thought wouldn't judge or make fun of her. Auntie is normally the person she would call but they are on the 'out' right now. Tonya feels completely lost in this moment and is fighting the flood of thoughts of an old faithful 'friend.']

(Sitting on the couch with a sea of used tissues surrounding her feet, Tonya begins a dialogue with herself) Ok...Ok... Tonya, this is NOT the end of the world. We have been single before and it's no big deal. I'm not gon' do like I have in the past and bust his windows or slash his tires. I'm not gon' call his job and pretend to be his baby momma and tell everybody he don't take care of his kids. I'm not gon' find him at his spot and show out...'cause I can SHOW OUT! Oh yes, I can. But I'm not (insert purposefully calm face with matching hand gestures) ...I'm gon' just let bruh gone on about his business (insert dismissive hand gestures). I ain't got time for cell block 8, OK!!! (insert widely opened eyes and a head slightly turned to the side). AND (insert long pause) ...I'm NOT going to get no ice cream. I'm gon' sit here, watch my movie and eat me another sausage sandwich. Matter of fact this time Imma put some mustard on it. Somebody told me mustard is good for heartburn and gas. We'll see.

(Tonya cooks the other half of the link and prepares two sausage sandwiches. Tonya finishes the remainder of the lemonade with the sandwiches and continues watching her movie.) Whew Chile! My chest burning, but it'll go away.

I want something sweet though... (Frowning her face in contemplation, she thinks of what she has that will satisfy her craving.) I'll just make me a piece of jelly toast. I already had four pieces today, but I need something to soak up this grease and satisfy this sweet tooth. (Tonya continues watching her movie and the heart burn has not gotten better with the jelly toast.) Oh God, please help me. This burning is ridiculous! It feel like when Prophet come down the prayer line and SLAP you in the chest so you can live right. (insert a swing of the arm to mimic Prophet) WHOP! Come on and live holy! (insert another swing) Whop! Come on and live righteous! I be like, bruh (insert aggressive body language and raised fists) ...You ain't got no more times to "come on" and do nothing wit' me. Slap me again and I promise you it ain't gon' be nothin 'nice! You gone see Peter rise up wit' that sword in the garden if you keep on playin' with me. Oh yes and Amen!!! I ain't gon' live by the sword but I will cut you, man of God. The Bible say touch NOT mine anointed. That's what it say, mm-hmm.

Let me see what's in this medicine cabinet. I gotta have something in there to help with this burning. (reaching the bathroom to search for antacid with no luck Tonya makes a decision) UUUGGGHHHH!! I ain't got nothin' in this house. I can't deal with this all night. I gotta go to the store. (Tonya throws on some clothes and heads to the store. She is a little self-conscious because her jeans are fitting a bit more snug than before and the thigh area is really wearing thin.)

[Tonya gets in her car and passes the oasis of fast food joints on her way to the Walmart®. She maintains her resolve NOT to get ice cream.]

Lord have mercy! Satan, I rebuke you in Jesus Name. EVERY-BODY wanna have signs for ice cream! Burger King got 50 cent cones! Checkers got swirl cones! McDonald's got $1 sundaes! Wendy's got Frosties! (slapping the steering wheel in frustration as she fights her temptation) Je-Sus! I'm tryna live right! I said I wasn't gettin' no doggone ice cream. Help Lord!! (Tonya begins to get angry at the onslaught of temptation on her way to the 24-hour Walmart®.)

(Tonya pulls into the store parking lot with a sigh of relief.) Whew!! (singing praises of Thanksgiving) Thank God I maaaaade it! (insert pious facial expression and a holy head shake) The devil thought he had me, BUT GOD! Hiya!!! He made a way! Oh yes, He did. (Tonya enters the store and goes straight to the pharmacy section and is surprised to see a familiar face.) Auntie!?!?!? What are you doing out this late? Are you ok?

Auntie: Lil gurl I got heart burn! Lord help today. It's killing me. I ain't been feeling good. I was in bed all day yesterday.

Tonya: (with sincere concern and care for Auntie, Tonya approaches and hugs her.) I got heart burn too, Auntie. I ate some swine Momma left at my house and it's been tragic ever since.

(The two collect their antacid tablets and begin to roam the store together chatting. Happy for the human interaction, they never address their recent quarrel. Auntie has a great idea.)

Auntie: I need to go 'head and get a few things while I'm in here. I didn't get out yesterday.

Tonya: Me too. I been so busy.

(The two gather their items and are heading toward the checkout past the frozen food section when Auntie remembers that she has a coupon in her purse.)

Auntie: Lord help today! I almost forgot.

Tonya: What, Auntie?

Auntie: I got a coupon that's about to expire. I don't wanna miss this good sale. (Auntie turns down the frozen food aisle leaving Tonya at the end.)

Tonya: For what? (as she watched Auntie walk away with her buggy)

Auntie: That good Blue Bell® ice cream! You know I gots to have my butter pecan. You know ice cream is good for heart burn. Milk help you when you got indigestions. That's why they call that medicine Milk of Magnesia. It taste like sin but it works.

Tonya: Say what?

Auntie: Yeah chile, milk good for all that stomach stuff.

Tonya: (Tonya turns her basket to follow Auntie and states her intentions) Well, I'm not getting no ice cream.

Auntie: (Auntie exclaims with tongues of praise and a holy dance when she reaches the ice cream section) Won't He do it?!?!??!

Tonya: (hurrying down the aisle to see what the excitement is about) What is it?

Auntie: Lil gurl they done rolled back the price! With my coupon, my gallon gone be $2. (insert tongues of thanksgiving and a holy shuffle of the feet) Yes God! I tell ya lil gurl, He keep on blessin' me.

Tonya: (Beginning to contemplate the purchase, she decides not to buy.) Oh, well that's nice but I don't have no coupon, so they not gon' get $4 outta me tonight.

Auntie: Oh, this a manufacturer's coupon. You can pull it up on your phone. Go 'head and see.

Tonya: (Tonya's eyes begin to survey the variety of the sweet cold treats and begins to think if she should make the purchase) No I'm good.

Auntie: Suit cho self, honey, I'm getting my butter pecan. I got some pound cake at home I need to finish.

Tonya: (Tonya sees that the store has single serve containers and begins to smile with a joyous look on her face) Oh look Auntie! They got the miniature size one. I'll just get that. That oughta be enough to knock out this heartburn.

[The two check out and part ways in the parking lot at midnight. Before she can crank her car, she has already opened the ice cream that conveniently came with a little spoon attached to the lid. Tonya eats half before pulling off to return home. Tonya takes the same route back home and begins to think about making a stop.]

Mm-mm-mm! Why did I come this way? I shoulda went down the other street. (While sitting at the stop light Tonya begins to justify why she needs to stop at one of the fast food locations.) Lord! My chest is still hurting. That lil bitty ice cream ain't touched NOTHIN up in here. (Looking at the container of antacid tablets, Tonya decides that she wants a more natural remedy.) I don't like taking medicine anyway. I like home remedies better. Pulling out her phone to check her account, Tonya sees her balance and decides that her purchase needs to be small.) Where all my money went?!?!? (insert surprised look) One account is overdrawn and the other one only got $20 in it. Good thing I got a half a tank and we get paid Friday. Imma have to look and see if somebody got into my account! I'll call the bank on Monday. (insert confused and angry facial expression) This don't make no sense. I know I had some money earlier this week. When I checked, I had $200 in one account and $79 in the other. Where is my money?!?!??!

(Tonya concludes that she needs to get the most for her money and decides to get a 4 for 4 meal from Wendy's.) That's ok, I'll just get old faithful. I'll go to the Wendy's by my job since the manager know me. He'll let me switch out my drink for a large frosty. That'll knock this heart burn out! And then I'll get them blessed nuggets, fries, and the cheeseburger. They fries are natural and they use sea salt so they waaaaay better than the other places.

[Tonya makes her purchase exactly as she planned and spends the car ride home balancing driving with eating her ice cream, fries, and nuggets interchangeably. Arriving back home at 1:30am, Tonya assumes her position on the couch, starts her movie over, and eats her cheeseburger with her Dr. Pepper because it was only an extra dollar. Tonya falls asleep on the couch while watching her movie and awakes Monday at 7:30 a.m.]

(Opening her eyes and wondering why it's so bright outside Tonya jumps up and checks her phone and finds that she is

> going to be late for work.) Lord have mercy!!! I ain't heard nan alarm!!! (Rushing to make herself presentable, she begins to talk down to herself about her behaviors and choices that led to this moment.)

...the cycle of bondage begins again. Let's dissect this scenario to see how Tonya got trapped AGAIN.

LET'S TALK ABOUT IT

In the last chapter we learned how Pride is a sneaky spirit that masks itself in opinions and preferences. In this chapter, we will look at temptation from the spiritual perspective and uncover how it manifested in the above scenario.

Temptation is defined by Merriam-Webster dictionary online (2020) as:

> "the act of tempting or the state of being tempted especially to evil :ENTICEMENT
>
> Synonyms for temptation - allurement, enticement, lure, seduction"

Cambridge Dictionary online (2020) defines temptation as:

1. "The desire to have or do something, especially something wrong, or something that causes desire.

2. the wish to do or have something that you know you should not do or have"

Having these definitions and commentary should help you to understand what temptation really is. We know that temptation does not come from God because it is an enticement toward evil and there is no darkness or variance in God (1 John 1:5; James 1:17). He cannot be light and dark (Matthew 12:24-25), so that leaves one source of temptation, Satan (the devil, the tempter). We must remember that though we have the thoughts in our mind, the desires in our heart, and the physical effects/symptoms of withdrawal, we are not dealing with a natural entity. Ephesians 6:12 informs us that our fight is not in the natural but in the Spirit. Therefore, if we are in a fight, we must put on our armor to protect us in the fight for our freedom (Ephesians 6:11). In the next chapter we will discuss what that looks like day to day.

Matthew 4:1-11 recounts Jesus being tempted in the wilderness and refers to Satan as the tempter. Knowing this and referring to the definitions and synonyms above, we can conclude that Satan has the ability to seduce, entice, lure, and set traps that incite us to desire things we know we should not have OR are wrong. There are a number of scriptures that speak of Satan's keen ability to affect the human psyche and choices. Genesis 3:1-15 teaches us how slick the enemy is and how he manipulates to gain control through our weaknesses and affect our resolve. Eve was deceived with a word...just like Tonya. After Tonya made a decision not to buy any ice cream, the seduction and alluring words of Auntie affected her mindset and she purchased a lesser amount thinking that her compromise was acceptable. The serpent is identified as the craftiest creature of all the beasts of the field (Genesis 3:1). This gives us an idea of his level of intelligence and deceitful skillset. If God's word makes a designation regarding a person, place, or thing, we know it's true because He is creator of ALL things; He is Elohim (the Lord our creator).

If Eve and Tonya had strong resolve to truly submit to the will of God, the enemy would have had no opportunity to ensnare them. James 4:7 says,

> "Submit yourselves, then, to God. Resist the devil, and he will flee from you." *(NIV)*

Submission is sometimes seen as a dirty word in the church, but I see it as a paradigm of protection. We should seek to submit every area of our lives to Abba. When we do so, we are covered and protected from harm in all areas. Our finances, relationships, marriages, work ethic, management of our home, our dietary consumption, raising our children, and allocation of our time should ALL be submitted to the perfect will of God. When our choice is to submit and serve God, our resolve is strengthened by the sure reward and safety of God's presence. We must learn to see God's hedge as a defense and not a denial that will bring great reward (James 1:12).

Luke 22:3 shows us that Satan is always looking for an opportunity to trip us up. However, our choices give him the permission to do so. The Holman Illustrated Bible Dictionary says this,

> "...Temptation may be for the purpose of destroying a person through sin leading to death and hell. This is Satan's intent. God may allow testing for the purpose of bringing forth faith and patience, which ultimately honor Him, as in the case of Job..." *(page 1568, 2003).*

When we are in line with the will of God, obeying His word, walking His path of righteousness, and exhibiting His character, we give no place to the devil. We are in position to remain covered under the shadow of his wings. BUT if we break a hedge we will be bitten (Ecclesiastes 10:8). Again, I say, God's parameters are in place to help, not hinder. The enemy, Satan, has no good intentions toward us. His desire is to steal, kill, and destroy (John 10:10). That was his purpose in the Garden and that is his purpose now. The satisfaction of fulfilling desire is momentary, but the results can persist for a lifetime.

Another method of resisting temptation is by being prepared. Tonya spent all day Saturday fulfilling the lusts of her flesh, shopping for attire to present an image at an event and did not take care of the needs of her home. Therefore, she fell 'off the wagon' of healthy eating and resorted to the binge foods she ate earlier in the week. She also did not purge her home of the foods that promote bondage. There should have been no cookies, pork rinds, swine, jelly, or lemonade in her home to 'fall back' on. Additionally, Tonya 'ate right' on Saturday to give herself permission to indulge on grits, eggs, bacon, corn beef hash, and toast. She already knew what she wanted to do and had all the supplies right there in her home. If we want to be free, we must be honest with ourselves about our choices and behaviors. If we continue to make excuses surrounding our cycles, we only deceive ourselves and prolong our deliverance. When we are truly submitted and resolved for change, we don't provide ourselves with the opportunity to fall. Tonya should have given her departing salutations to Auntie when she saw her go down the frozen section. Tonya has visited that specific Walmart® many times and knows what's on every aisle. She succumbed to the desire that was already in her heart. Her will was not strong enough at that time to resist being surrounded by a plethora of ice cream options. That aisle was a trap for sure. Here's another point to make - just because someone is an authority figure, elder, or carries a title doesn't mean that they have the resolve you do in certain areas. If their life does not match your choices in an area, you should seek counsel elsewhere. Tonya allowed the deceptive words Auntie used to convince herself that her choice was acceptable to invade her ear gates and plant seeds that quickly grew to become a foul vineyard that instantly brought forth intoxicating wine to change her mind.

Matthew 11:12 talks about the violent insurgence of the enemy that comes against the kingdom of God. I submit to you that you must have the same intensity for your freedom as the intensity of the enemy to ensnare you. When Joseph served Potiphar and his wife continually attempted to seduce him, that brother ran so hard that he came out of his clothes and left it there. This is the resolve we must have if we are truly seeking freedom. Why would Tonya take the same route back home? She knew every restaurant and fast food joint in proximity to her home. Would you like to know what happened? When Tonya purchased that miniature portion of ice cream the door of temptation opened, and a flood of desire came in. It was like the levees breaking on a dam and flooding a city. Once the door was open, all the desires in her soul began to work together to get more of what they wanted. Let's view Tonya's progression:

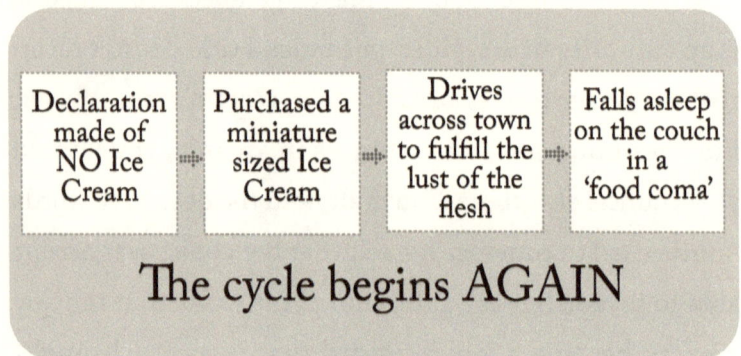

Her desire became so strong that she drove across town to the location she knew would meet her lust. She not only wasted more monetary resources, but the resource of time, gas, and health. If she was still having heartburn, and had the medicine to 'cure' it, why did she still go to Wendy's? I heard Pastor Voddie Bauchum say this years ago,

> "If the wisest man in the world *(Solomon)*, the strongest man in the world *(Sampson)*, and the most devout man in the world *(David)* all fell into temptation, what makes us think that we have a chance?" *(paraphrased)* [youtube video: Title - Voddie Baucham - Love and Marriage (Full Series: Sermons Only) Channel - Bosco Tung].

Please take these wise words to heart. Do not think your strength is enough to combat the enemy's insurgence on your soul. We must lean and depend upon the Father to grace us to endure through the onslaught of the enemy. God's strength is made perfect in our weakness, and we must not only recognize our weakness but proclaim them so we can be covered in the power of God to resist what further weakens us (2 Corinthians 12:9, NIV).

Abba only wants to see us succeed, but we must be willing and obedient participants in His plan to bring us to freedom.

LET'S WORK THROUGH THIS TOGETHER

Prompts:

1. What about Tonya's behaviors reminds you of yourself?

   _____
   _____
   _____
   _____

2. Tonya chose fast food over financial stability. Describe a scenario where you placed the satisfaction of a craving over practicality.

   _____
   _____
   _____
   _____

3. Think about the strongest temptation you've ever had regarding food. Were you successful in resisting the temptation? Explain Why or Why not?

   _____
   _____
   _____
   _____

4. List below the foods that are temptations for you (i.e. your 'favorite' foods). Write how long it's been since you've been tempted with that food item. If you consume the item on a regular basis, draw a line through it.

_____
_____
_____
_____

5. In a week's time (7 days), how often do you fall into temptation? Why do you think you fall so often?

_____
_____
_____
_____

6. Think back, how often have you allowed the words and counsel of others to deter, dismantle, and disrupt your plans to change your life? Why do you think the words of this person or people were so powerful?

_____
_____
_____
_____

7. Do you really want change? Why?

_____
_____
_____

Encouragement:

Ladies and gentlemen, please know that Abba loves you so much that He wants to see you free! The enemy only wants to further bind you and bring you into deeper places, pits of despair and bondage. Knowing this, we can trust in Abba's instructions, understanding that they are bringing us to a promised place. Jeremiah 29:11 says,

> "'For I know the plans I have for you,' declares the LORD, 'plans to prosper you and not to harm you, plans to give you hope and a future.'" *(NIV)*

God's word is full of His promises for His children. We have never gone far enough that God's LOVE can't bring us back. Trust Him, believe Him, and know that submitting to His Perfect Will will always bring you toward hope and help for change to reach your future.

Prayer:

Abba,

I thank you for your unfailing Love and your ears being inclined toward me. I thank you for your peace and your rest. I thank you for your protection and the hedges you have placed around my life. Teach me how to surrender my desires. Teach me how to resist the devil so he flees from me. Teach me how to use my armor so I can remain protected in the battle. Abba, I love you and I want to serve you from a free place. Help me...I have faith that you will.

In Jesus Name,
Amen

Walk it Out

I am aware that *everyone* is not called to veganism. Others don't desire to be vegan. This journal is to inform the masses of the process of deliverance the Father lovingly walked me through to bring me to a place of freedom, wholeness, and health. Returning to Abba's original agenda set forth in the garden for our dietary needs SAVED my natural and Spiritual life! I was on the road toward a lifetime of pain and pills until Abba grabbed my attention. In fact, He informed me that He HEALED my body of the ailments I suffered through my obedience to the disciplines He set before me. I did not take any supplements, drink any shakes, pop any pills, sprinkle any powder on my food, take any miracle wonder drug, rub any cream on my skin, wrap myself in any products, or have surgery. I simply submitted to the call to be set apart, surrendered my will for His, obeyed His instruction EVERY step of the way, and the result is freedom. Freedom that has brought me to the place where I can now pour into the lives of others and help them journey toward the promised land.

Over the course of one week, we have taken a journey through the lives of Tonya and Auntie. We have studied their behavior patterns, identified triggers, and the progression of bondage that strengthens strongholds. My hope and my prayer are that through our study and your journaling, you have come to a decision that change must happen AND that NOW is the time!

This chapter is designed to give you the tools and strategies needed to combat the desire to return to the old way of life. These are the tools I used to combat the enemy and war for my freedom by the grace of God. First, I did NOTHING in my power. I leaned and depended upon Him with every step and at every intersection. Remember, if Samson, David, and Solomon fell into temptation, you can too. Remain humble and trust Abba to usher you into the promised land.

If we are in a battle for freedom, there are certain items we need to be successful. David carried a slingshot and five smooth stones (1 Samuel 17:40, BSB), Samson had the jawbone of a donkey (Judges 51:16, ESV), and Jeremiah had a Spiritual war club (Jeremiah 51:20, NIV); in the natural those building the wall with Jeremiah carried a tool in one hand and a spear in the other (Nehemiah 4:17, ISV). These mighty men of valor were experienced in battle, with skill sets the new soldier is yet to obtain. Therefore, wisdom says more protection is needed.

Ephesians 6:11; 10-18 speaks about the armor of God and its importance to those who enter a war zone. We have learned that the enemy ONLY wants to steal, kill, and destroy. Satan is forever seeking an opportunity to trap the believer and desires to keep us in bondage. It is imperative to your warfare strategy to remember that he spends all his time going to and fro looking for someone to devour (1 Peter 5:8). That means you must be on guard, protected, and ready at all times. This is why armor is important. Let's see what Abba has prepared for our protection:

Helmet of Salvation

Identity is foundational to the life of the believer. Do you know who you are? Do you know who you belong to? If you did, the thoughts the enemy uses to ensnare us would be identified and cast down. The security of knowing that you are a child of the King is priceless. When we have identity, we don't allow anyone, including the devil or ourselves, to label us as anything other than that. Remember that words have power. God spoke a word and all of creation came into existence (Psalm 33:9). The mind is the epicenter of the body. Your mind is so powerful that the thoughts we have can invoke a response in our physical body (Proverbs 14:30).

Before a word is spoken, it is a thought. When the people of the earth began to build the tower of Babel (Gen

11:1-9), it began as a thought. The thought was birthed and then the idea came from their mouths. What you think, then speak has the power to affect your atmosphere positively or negatively. What you think, then speak will bring either death or life (Proverbs 18:21). What you think, then speak creates the world you live in. Be sure your helmet stays on to block the blows of the enemy against your mind.

Breastplate of Righteousness

Proverbs 4:23 speaks of the importance of guarding your heart. There are many versions of the Bible and each one speaks to individuals on the levels they can comprehend. Here are a few that I feel will drive the point home:

> Good News Translation "Be careful how you think; your life is shaped by your thoughts."
>
> New International Version "Above all else, guard your heart, for everything you do flows from it."
>
> King James Bible "Keep thy heart with all diligence; for out of it *are* the issues of life."
>
> GOD'S WORD® Translation "Guard your heart more than anything else, because the source of your life flows from it."

After viewing these versions of the scripture, it is clear that we must be intensely intentional about guarding our hearts. As stated in the above scriptures, it is the source of our life, thoughts, and everything. Our heart governs how we deal with our issues, ourselves, and one another. Ezekiel 36:26 tells us how important it is for us to have a soft heart and not one of stone. Our heart determines the quality of our relationships and our life. We can't expect to have healthy relationships when we have a boulder occupying the place of our heart. We must surrender to the tenderizing of our heart if we want an audience with God and relationship with man. Both are paramount to our existence in the earth and healing process.

Belt of Truth

The truth makes you free (John 8:32). Ponder how exacerbating it would be to walk around all day pulling up your skirt or pants all day long. If your pants were falling down, it would alter the way you walk, prevent you from moving effectively, and cause constant interruptions. Have you ever heard the saying that if you tell a lie that you have to continue telling lies to cover up the original lie? This is why having our core wrapped in truth is vital. The core of our body is the portion that 'holds it all together.' If we had no torso, we would be arms, legs, and a head...that's out of order!!!

Sword of the Spirit

Swords are a well-known weapon of warfare. It has the ability to cut many things, including cut through flesh. As you read, see YOURSELF through the lens of the scripture. Don't compare yourself to others or use the word to become judge, jury, and executioner to those who have harmed you. Allow it to cut away the dead things and baggage you carry. Allow it to cut away the soul ties, chains, and fetters that have kept you in bondage for so long. Allow the word to extract the dead places in you so that you can heal and become a whole, healthy individual. Allow the word of God to dissect you and expose every hidden place of brokenness. The goal is to be COMPLETELY healed; so, let the word work.

Feet Prepared with the Gospel of Peace

Psalms 119:105 speaks of the word of God being a lamp to our feet and a light to our path. How effective would you be at driving at night if you had no headlights? The journey toward freedom is new territory for you. You have not been here before, so you need light to help you see the way. The word of God is imperative to your success at remaining focused on the journey. Remember, the word of God is what Jesus used when the enemy tempted Him in the wilderness. If Jesus had the wisdom to say, "It is written…," we should follow His example. When we know who we are and what we have access to as the word of God states, we can be in peace, walk in peace, love in peace, and live in peace; with others and with ourselves.

Shield of Faith

This shield is so important because it blocks what the enemy launches at you. Think about a knight and the full body armor worn in battle. The armor was made of metal so if stones or arrows are launched and the armor takes on damage it becomes weak and much less effective. This is the importance of the shield. Think of the Roman soldiers of antiquity. They had no armor; they were equipped with spears or swords and a shield. The shield can withstand fire, quench arrows, and block stones. We need the shield to round out our protection.

Now that we have thoroughly studied our armor, let us take a look at what we can do to help our armor remain in pristine condition.

Daily Affirmations

2 Corinthians 5:17 teaches us that as we continually hear the word of God, our faith increases. Remember that Faith is your shield of protection. As you read, learn, study, and grow in understanding of the word of God, the size of your shield will increase and provide greater protection. God has graciously given all of us a portion of faith (Romans

12:3). Because faith is likened unto a seed (Matthew 17:20), that means it can grow. Frequent watering with the word will bring forth a great harvest.

Find scriptures that speak directly to you and your situation. Post them on your mirror, keep them in your car, download an app and keep them in your phone for ease of access. Whenever you have a moment, read and say them aloud. Before long, you will remember them without the aid of the cards, and you will have built an arsenal against the enemy.

Purge Your Pantry

Get rid of the junk! Tonya fell back into the cycle of eating junk after a day of success because she was not prepared, and she had the weapons of mass destruction in her pantry. Make it inconvenient for you to falter. Keep healthy, whole foods in your home, car, and at work. BE PREPARED!!!! It is YOUR responsibility to ensure that you have the foods that promote health and wellness. No one else is responsible to 'make sure' you live right. Make the choice and take the time to be prepared.

Run for Your Life!

Maintain a healthy distance from people, places, and things that bring temptation or present triggers. Lamentations 3:40 and Psalm 119:59 speak of us examining ourselves and turning away from the ways that lead to sin and destruction. You know exactly who, what, when, where, and how you get into trouble. If not, study yourself, be honest, and make the necessary changes. In my life of addiction, I knew exactly who to call when I wanted a good hardy binge session. I knew where all the deals were, what days the specials were on, I knew what staff people would do a lil something extra for me, and I knew how to navigate my city to feed my flesh with specific flavor profiles.

I also made the decision to turn away from relationships with fellow addicts. My goal was to be free, and anyone who had not made the same decision was a risk for me to engage with. A person I was in relationship with previously became angry with me because, as I began my journey, I refused to go out and eat with them as I had in the past. This person was upset and began to question me about why I was making changes. It was to the point that I had to become militant and state that my life had shifted, and I was no longer on that path. Needless to say, our lives began to separate in that very moment.

I was strategic in the provision of my flesh. So, as I took the time to study to know how to fulfill the lusts of my flesh, I made the same and greater efforts to save my life. You can do the same.

Here's an example of what that might look like:

Scene: Sitting at the table for a birthday gathering talking to yourself as the buffet line is being set up.

Get it together, girl. Mmm-mmm-mmm...Lord have Mercy!!! Why did I even walk up in this place? They got beans, greens, potatoes, tomatoes, fried chicken, baked spaghetti with cheese on top, smothered sausages, and everything I like on my plate. Well, I used to like. I'm living right now, though. Weeeell...I been livin' right, but I don't think it will hurt to have one slice of pie. No, no, no!! I've been doing good and I'm not turning back; I'm moving ahead. Yeah! That'll do it. I can just sing some praise and worship while I'm here, and I don't have to think about that big dish of mac 'n cheese they just brought out. Uuuuuugggghhhhh! Why did I come here??? I had to, right? I mean, I was invited. How could I not come? We've been friends for umpteen years, and she has always been there for me. We are practically family. I had to come...right? Anyway, here we go. 🎵Every praise is to our God. Every🎵...Lord help today!!! They just brought out a 4-layer homemade red velvet cake with cream cheese frosting and a peach cobbler. Uhn-uh!!! I got to go. <Hurriedly walks over to friend> Hey hun! I'm so happy for you reaching your milestone. You know I love you dearly. I'm so sorry I can't stay. I left your gift on the table. Let's chat and sync schedules so we can meet up and celebrate. Ok, hun! Love you, bye!

LOL...the moral here is to recognize where you are in your journey. Everyone isn't called to what you are called to. You have to be honest with yourself and know what you can and cannot handle in THIS season. Don't walk into situations where you know you will be tempted in the very area where you're seeking healing and deliverance. Alcoholics Anonymous members don't go to bars, so you shouldn't go to places where your vice (FOOD) will be abundantly present. Know your boundaries and respect them.

Remember to always PRAY your way through:

Abba,

I thank you that I have an intercessor in Christ. Nothing that I encounter is new or extraordinary. Because He has overcome the world and everything in it, so can I. Thank you.

It is so in Jesus Name, Amen

Social Media Cleanse

The age of technology is wonderful, we have almost everything at our fingertips. However, this is not the best thing for an addict. Tonya was plagued by thoughts of donuts after receiving a coupon from an app SHE downloaded on her phone. It's time to PURGE!!!! Clear out your social media. When walking through my healing and deliverance process, I unfollowed everything that brought reminders of the foods that were no longer acceptable for me. I deleted apps, unsubscribed from email lists, and even unfriended a few people. I also limited, and at times eliminated, the use of social media. I was too sensitive to play with that thing! I was determined to be free at ALL costs. Are you determined? Make the change!

Identify Your Triggers

Prayerfully, having reached the end of the journal means that you have sincerely worked through the process of identifying your triggers. Take time to study yourself further with the assistance of the Holy Spirit as your guide. He is our helper (John 14:26) and will lead you into all truth (John 16:13). Trust in Him and He will teach you how to know yourself on a deeper level.

Learn the Names of God

Many families have the practice of using nicknames or pet names. The use of specific names generally speaks to the level of intimacy you have with a person. The relationship, and your function therein, is often determined by the name you use. When we call Abba by His names, it makes us, creation, and Him aware of the specific character trait we need in that moment. Of course, we know that God knows everything, but when we use His names, it is an act of faith and agreement with the attributes, power, and authority related to that Name.

Many names of God have been used in this journal, but here are a few more of my favorites:

> Jehovah Gibbor - The Mighty God
>
> El Shaddai - The all sufficient One
>
> El ELyon - The Most High God
>
> Adonai - God is my Lord

These are just a few of the names of God. Study the scriptures and learn more to build your arsenal. Study the use of the names in scripture, memorize them, and begin to use them in your daily language and prayer life. You will notice the difference.

Study the Word of God

Reading is not studying. I can read something through to check it off my list and not retain an ounce of the content. To study means to read with intention, reflect and meditate on what's read, look for complementary texts, seek further explanation, and gain greater understanding. Study to show yourself approved. Remember, the serpent perverted the word of God. If you KNOW what it says, you will know when it is perverted. STUDY!

Resources

Here are a few resources that will help you study. Type the links into your browser, and there you will gain access to a wealth of knowledge on the scriptures including a plethora of versions of the Bible, commentaries, articles, Greek, Hebrew, reading plans, programs, and text comparison:

https://www.blueletterbible.org/

https://www.biblegateway.com/

https://biblehub.com/

https://www.youversion.com/

Continue Journaling

We have the Bible because men were inspired by God to chronicle the events of History in the natural and in the Spirit. I'm so glad they did! The Bible has been my teacher, friend, and source of discipline on this journey and in daily life. Take the time to write daily. It will help you:

- Decompress throughout or at the end of the day
- Track success
- Study failures
- Build faith as you review your progress
- Become a source of encouragement as you walk closer toward your promised land of freedom.

Celebrate Your Successes

Acknowledge your progress, continue praying, and celebrate your milestones. Here's an example of what that might look like:

> Whew Chile!!! I did it...I made it through. I can't believe it. I actually made it through the day without meat. I didn't stop at Publix for no spicy wings. I didn't go to Salem's for a Philly and fries. I didn't go to Zeko's for no fried fish with rice, beans, and chop chop. I didn't even go to the 7Eleven® to get my spicy pork rinds and a cookie. HALLELUJAH! Won't He do it!?!?
>
> I actually can do all things through Christ who gives me strength. (Philippians 4:13)

Prayer

Father,

I stand in faith agreement with your word over my life. I believe your word is true. I CAN do this with you leading and guiding me. I trust you.

In Jesus Name, Amen

Find other ways to reward yourself that don't involve food. Surround yourself with people that are positive influences and want to see you successful and free. You have a great future ahead of you. Take everything you've learned and ready your armor and assemble your book of strategies. YOU WILL WIN because GOD NEVER FAILS!

Next Steps

NOW! *You've done great* work, and it's time to move to the next phase while you are motivated and ready. It's time to fast. Fasting brings the Spirit, soul, and body into alignment. It weakens fleshly desires and elevates the spirit man while helping the body to detox from the past. I recommend that you seek God about how He desires you to fast and what He is requiring of you in this season.

Thee Gold Standard, LLC has a fasting guide, **Liquid Gold**, specifically designed to assist you with transitioning to the next phase of your healing and deliverance. The **Liquid Gold** guide is equipped with commentary, thought provoking journal prompts, and recipes to ease the transition. Pick up a copy today!

References

abuse. 2020. In *Merriam-Webster.com*. Retrieved March 7, 2020, from https://www.merriam-webster.com/dictionary/abuse

Draper, C. and Brand, C. (2003). *The Holman Illustrated Bible Dictionary*. Nashville, TN: Holman Reference

Silver, N. (2018, January 17). *How long can you live without food?* Retrieved from https://www.healthline.com/health/food-nutrition/how-long-can-you-live-without-food#bodily-response

Janiszewski, P. (2015, December 2). *How long can humans survive without food or water?* Retrieved from https://medicalxpress.com/news/2015-12-humans-survive-food.html

integrity. 2020. In *Merriam-Webster.com*. Retrieved March 7, 2020, from https://www.merriam-webster.com/dictionary/integrity

temptation. 2020. In *Merriam-Webster.com*. Retrieved March 7, 2020, from https://www.merriam-webster.com/dictionary/temptation

temptation. 2020. In *Dictionary.Cambridge.org*. Retrieved March 7, 2020, from https://dictionary.cambridge.org/us/dictionary/english/temptation

Notes Page

Notes Page

Notes Page

Notes Page

www.ingramcontent.com/pod-product-compliance
Lightning Source LLC
Chambersburg PA
CBHW030553080526
44585CB00012B/366